THE
FOURTH
MOON

THE FOURTH MOON

A STEP-BY-STEP PROCESS FOR
SUSTAINABLE
BUSINESS SUCCESS

DARREN K. BOURKE

EMERALD
BOOK CO.

Published by Emerald Book Company
Austin, TX
www.emeraldbookcompany.com

Distributed by Emerald Book Company

For ordering information or special discounts for bulk purchases, please contact
Emerald Book Company at PO Box 91869, Austin, TX 78709, 512.891.6100.

Design and composition by Greenleaf Book Group and Kim Lance
Cover design by Greenleaf Book Group and Kim Lance
Interior images received from Galileo are posted on the World Wide Web, on the Galileo mission home page at URL http://galileo.jpl.nasa.gov/. Background information and educational context for the images can be found at http://www.jpl.nasa.gov/galileo/sepo.

Cataloging-in-Publication data is available.

ISBN 13: 978-1-937110-69-7

Part of the Tree Neutral® program, which offsets the number of trees consumed in the production and printing of this book by taking proactive steps, such as planting trees in direct proportion to the number of trees used: www.treeneutral.com

Printed in the United States of America on acid-free paper

15 16 17 18 19 20   10 9 8 7 6 5 4 3 2 1

First Edition

Other Edition(s)
eBook ISBN: 978-1-937110-70-3

To my beautiful wife and best friend, Jan.

Your love, belief, and support has been my compass
on the journey to our Fourth Moon.

CONTENTS

Discovering the Fourth Moon

In this book, I show how any business can reach optimal and sustainable success. I do this by using a powerful metaphor based on Galileo Galilei, the famous Italian astronomer, and the four moons of Jupiter. Through this metaphor and through the journey of business owner Tom Dylan and his team, I will demonstrate time-tested, proven, and easy-to-implement success strategies for achieving spectacular success.

As you will discover in the pages ahead, commencing your journey and reaching each of the four moons sequentially is a practical step-by-step process that any business owner and his or her team can implement. Like anything worthwhile in life, there is always commitment and effort required. Knowing isn't doing; you have to commit to the same habits and disciplines, and repeat them over and over again. However, if you are open to learning and committing to specific habits and disciplines, you too can reach the Fourth Moon.

The good news for you, reader, is that the Fourth Moon metaphor is simple, elegant, and proven. Once you understand the underlying principles, you and your team can immediately implement these within your business by following a step-by-step process.

The characters and case studies used throughout the book are fictitious and drawn from the hundreds and hundreds of businesses I have worked with and learned from over the years. And in the final pages of this book, I will direct you to important resources to help you launch your journey to the Fourth Moon.

As of today, I've worked with nearly a thousand businesses, experience that has taught me a great deal about what it takes to succeed in business and in life. But how did I even get started with this Fourth Moon business? Where did the idea come from? To help you get a sense for the background of this one-of-a-kind approach, I want to share the short version of my path to my own Fourth Moon.

THE JUNIOR ENTREPRENEUR

As a kid, I remember being fascinated by people, language, and words. And of course, numbers.

I spent hours watching and listening to people. Studying their mannerisms and remembering their faces. I loved being a people-watcher. Human beings are by far the most important, fascinating, and perplexing objects in existence. Some people are obsessed with history or geography. But for me it is human beings. This interest in people has led me to acquire an uncanny, almost photographic ability to remember people's faces. I consistently recognize people from all aspects of my life, often as far back as when I was a young child.

I was also fascinated by language and words, or more particularly phrases, sayings, and colloquialisms—those wonderful colorful word strings that adults would use to make a point. Slang and rhyming slang also captivated me. I would hear adults come out with these clever and hilarious sayings and commit them to memory. I'd then wait for the opportunity to drop them into discussion in just the right context. I recall my young friends sometimes laughing at me and telling me I'd made these phrases up. More often than not, they'd check with their parents after school and report back the next day reluctantly admitting the phrase I'd quoted did in fact exist. I would go home quite chuffed at these verbal victories. I confess to having taken this sport to a higher level as an adult—crafting my own phrases and analogies. It's fun and makes people smile. Makes them think.

Numbers were my other love. I loved the way in which numbers interacted with each other and the world around me. Calculating sports scores, handling money, and adding/multiplying/subtracting/dividing numbers were practiced and honed at school and home. I still believe those four buttons on a calculator are the most important to understand. They're all you need to know about mathematics in business.

I can vaguely remember my first entrepreneurial experience. Our neighbors were apple growers and they needed some help picking up the "windies." The windies were the apples that had been blown off the tree by the wind. While bruised and unsuitable for eating, they could be used for juicing. The task was set for me to work through the orchard picking up the apples from the ground and placing them in wooden boxes. I'm told by my parents that I worked diligently for quite some time over that weekend. After my work was through, I discovered to my surprise that I had been paid a fixed price per box filled. This was extremely exciting to a young boy, and I pocketed my earnings with great pride.

The apple experience led on to several other early entrepreneurial ventures. My father taught me how to mow our lawns as well as general troubleshooting of the lawn mower. With these skills, I was able to offer mowing services to my neighbors, who were more than happy to employ me. A car-washing service soon followed. School provided a market for selling sports fan merchandise, where I learned to buy wholesale and sell retail.

Extensive residential housing development in our neighborhood led to a proliferation of recyclable aluminum cans and glass bottles left on housing lots by thirsty builders. This opportunity provided me and my childhood mates with a rich vein of moneymaking recyclables right in our own backyard. The trick was to get on site quickly at the end of the working day after the builders left. I still remember sitting on the family couch and watching a TV advertisement telling us that the recycling return deposit on bottles was doubling. I couldn't believe my ears. My large stock of bottles had just doubled in price overnight. I was elated.

THE ADOLESCENT APPRENTICESHIP

The adolescent years were dominated by sport, social activity, and casual employment. As soon as I could get a casual job, I was there. An attitude of "why not" led me into casual and vacation employment in supermarkets, IT distribution, textile warehousing, hospitality, and even road construction.

I happily did everything and anything to gain experience. I even negotiated with my high school to do a work experience placement two years in a row, when only one year's placement is the norm. I craved experience and thrived on learning new skills and industry knowledge. The greatest gift this adolescent apprenticeship gave me was the skill to be able to communicate and build rapport from the cleaner to the CEO.

The other turning point was the opportunity to attend corporate training as a seventeen-year-old. My father was employed by IBM and was attending an in-house training course. The course was based on new-age thinking to achieving your potential, compiled and delivered by the legendary Lou Tice. The material was very state-of-the-art in the mid-1980s and introduced me to positive thinking, affirmations, visualization techniques, and so much more. It was a watershed moment for me, and I studied the techniques diligently, resulting in the dramatic improvement of my grades and achievements over the next six months of my final school year.

THE ADULT APPRENTICESHIP

I still remember the day. I had nearly completed my commerce degree at the University of Melbourne. The hottest job to get offered was a graduate position with the prestigious "Big 8" international chartered accounting firms. I can still recall the envelope arriving in the mail and taking private sanctuary in the household toilet to open it. To my amazement, it was a job offer from Deloitte—one of the prestigious firms. I was in!

That ticket led me to get paid to learn, observe, and assist businesses of all different sizes and contrasting industries on a daily basis. How lucky was I? My accounting career gave me exposure to hundreds of businesses and culminated in becoming a manager of a team of accountants. While this stage of my career had been incredibly educational, challenging, and rewarding—the entrepreneurial voice inside kept calling me.

There were two things at play at this stage of my career. First, I felt my outgoing personality and style were being constrained and compromised within the confines of a professional services firm. Secondly, the entrepreneur's voice was getting louder. My mind was constantly occupied by ideas, thoughts, and visions of breaking free and starting my own business.

THE APPRENTICE BREAKS FREE

At age thirty-one, I busted out.

As part of my chartered accounting role, I had completed training in recruitment, conducted graduate recruitment, recruited industry positions for clients, and managed a young team of accountants. I enjoyed developing these skills and felt I had a natural flair for identifying and recruiting talent.

As a result, a fellow manager and I decided to break out on our own and start a recruitment agency specializing in finance personnel. Taking up a serviced office in the central business district, we had no clients, no jobs, and six months of cash burn. Luckily, we survived this start-up phase and became known for our consultative approach to recruitment. We were accountants recruiting accountants. We knew our market, and it was fun and exciting. Heady days!

After six years, I sold out my interest to my partner and took a twelve-month sabbatical. This period, and the resultant search for my next venture, was one of the most challenging stages of my life.

I had exposure to hundreds of businesses, had recruited hundreds of people, and had navigated my way through my first serious entrepreneurial venture. However, I honestly didn't know what was next. I knew what I didn't want. I didn't want to work in a gray office. I wanted to be authentic and do something special—something that really mattered to both the people I served and to me.

MY DISCOVERY

Out of a searching sabbatical year finally came clarity. What if I were to be authentic and fulfill my desire to help people? What if I worked from home and saw my family? I could set up a business my way, work with people I respected, do great things with them, and operate on my terms. It was a lightbulb moment.

I thought of all the things that annoyed clients of professional service firms. And I reversed them. I would charge fixed fees. I would cap the number of clients I worked with. I would deliver exceptional personalized service. I would consult, coach, and mentor privately owned small and medium-sized businesses.

In my work, business owners explain to me they want to move from A to B. This might involve tangibles such as money, people, time, or resources. Alternatively, it might involve intangibles such as stress, reputation, relationships, or satisfaction. I would then help these clients focus on their key priorities (described as Mission Goals in the book) and facilitate them toward achieving their goals and dreams.

I am so fortunate they pay me to do this work that I love so dearly. For me, there is nothing more satisfying than helping an individual or team succeed.

WHICH LEADS ME TO THE FOURTH MOON . . .

I'll let you learn about the Fourth Moon as you read ahead. But for the moment, a little bit of background won't hurt.

As I filled my coaching business with clients under my own leveraged model, I was able to quarantine time for other important activities. Not being part of the rat race allowed me to fertilize an open mind and continue my commitment to a lifetime of learning. I made time available to study philosophy, meditation, marketing, nonfiction writing, screenwriting, digital media, speaking, and publishing.

I also dedicated over four years to volunteer mentoring for the Reach Foundation. The Reach Foundation was jointly founded by Jim Stynes and aims to help at-risk youth pursue their dreams. I was involved in programs, workshops, business incubators, and one-to-one mentoring to help youth pursue their business dreams.

And finally, you are reading this book because of the discovery of my Fourth Moon. Without my discovery, I would never have had the vision, inspiration, and time to create this important message and put it into print.

For me, this book is the culmination of decades of commitment, work, and learning. The Fourth Moon is a destination I cherish and want to share with the world.

For you, I hope you enjoy this book, understand its key messages, and start a journey to your Fourth Moon.

The Insights of a Famous Italian Astronomer

The discovery of the four moons of Jupiter changed man's relationship with the universe. Believe it or not, it is also the discovery that will ultimately transform your business and personal life. As we travel together to the Fourth Moon through the pages of this book, you will undergo a transformation in your relationship to your business that will be as breathtaking as space travel.

Our journey begins in the laboratory of a scientific genius. Gazing into the night sky with a powerful telescope of his own creation, Galileo Galilei was the first human to see it. The seventeenth-century Italian astronomer, physicist, mathematician, and philosopher was searching for proof—proof that the planets in our solar system revolved around the sun, not the earth. All the major institutions of the day actively opposed Galileo's belief in the "heliocentric view" of the universe as postulated a century earlier by the astronomer Copernicus.

But Galileo believed that the benefits of discovering the truth far outweighed the costs of accepting a popular misconception.

One evening in 1610, Galileo spotted them: three heavenly bodies close to Jupiter. Amazingly, the next night he even spotted a fourth. At first he wasn't sure if the four heavenly bodies supported his theory. Only after several days of careful study did he determine that the bodies actually orbited Jupiter. The Galilean moons, as they were later called, disproved the prevailing theory of the day: that all heavenly bodies circled the earth. From that moment on, science was free to explore the full potential of the cosmos.

In commerce, as in science, we must understand basic truths in order to bring about desired results. Just as the discovery of the Galilean moons laid the groundwork for the growth of modern science, your discovery of the Fourth Moon will enable you to realize the growth and financial success that you have only imagined.

Are you ready to discover the Fourth Moon? Let's begin.

WHAT THE DISCOVERY OF THE GALILEAN MOONS HAS IN COMMON WITH BUSINESS SUCCESS

Galileo possessed three important attitudes that assisted him on his path to discovery.

First, he went into his investigation with patience, not knowing exactly what he would discover, but with the commitment to make detailed and painstaking observations. Jupiter's moons were a surprise. You, too, will require the patience to make detailed observations about your business.

Second, he took careful observations, from which he drew conclusions with an open mind. His discovery disproved geocentrism. You, too, will have to review your observations with an open mind and be prepared to draw unexpected conclusions.

And third, he persevered with his conclusions despite the opposition of the leaders of his time. You, too, will have to persevere, sometimes contrary to the views of others, to reach your Fourth Moon.

Patience. Open-mindedness. Perseverance.

Imagine the patience required of Galileo in conducting his nightly observations. After all, up until the night of his discovery, the four moons were undiscovered celestial bodies. His discovery was completely unanticipated.

Most of us struggle to maintain patience in seeking a known outcome. But the patience required to search for an unknown object or phenomenon is unfathomable.

The strength of belief in the geocentric view in the seventeenth century was overwhelming. The theory that Earth was the center of the universe sat perfectly with the Church, the State, and the ego of humankind. Galileo's willingness to adopt a view contrary to this universally accepted theory shows the brilliance of the man, particularly when he was able to prove it was completely and gloriously wrong!

Of course his discovery of the four moons not only challenged the accepted wisdom of the time, but even more acutely it challenged the authority of religious and political leaders. Despite irrefutable evidence, his amazing discovery unwittingly put him at odds with the powerful Roman Catholic Church. He faced a Roman Inquisition, and despite being cleared of any offense, he was condemned by the Church to recant, and was held under house arrest for the rest of his life—some eight years. The level of perseverance required to hold on to his beliefs in the face of this demonization and persecution would have broken most mortals.

Have you ever ignored new information or a different perspective that challenged one of your long-held beliefs? There are many people who will challenge your views despite the evidence or research you may have to support them. Critical family members, friends, or business associates can stop you from taking action and pursuing your dreams and goals. Partners, employees, and suppliers may not share your vision. Financiers, advisers, and government departments aren't in the business of risk taking and can stifle—even kill—your entrepreneurial spirit, if you allow them.

Just like Galileo, you need to be strong, even if it means being contrarian, as you follow through with the strategies and disciplines that are linked to your success.

ADOPTING GALILEO'S ATTITUDES

As a business owner you need to adopt Galileo's attitudes of patience, open-mindedness, and perseverance.

With patience, you can make powerful observations from which to draw revolutionary conclusions. With open-mindedness, you can reengineer your business without self-imposed or external limitations holding you back. Of course this reengineering will come with the typical challenges of change management. But tenacious perseverance will carry you and your business beyond these teething problems.

Regardless of your industry or the size of your business, there are principles of success that are universal. Combining Galileo's attitudes with time-tested and proven strategies, I'll show you how to travel to Galileo's four moons in order to strategize, implement, maintain, and—most importantly—leverage your success. All you have to do is join me on a journey to the Fourth Moon.

THE STRUCTURE OF THIS BOOK

Soon you will be introduced to Tom Dylan, owner of Dylan IT, whom I will be taking on a life-changing journey to the Fourth Moon. If Tom can ultimately reach the Fourth Moon, a universe of unlimited opportunity awaits. But he must be prepared to commit to the journey and navigate its course.

To help you get to know and recall the individuals who work with Tom at Dylan IT, I will use throughout the book nicknames based on each employee's role within the company:

Name and Role	Nickname
Jimmy–Operations Manager	Jimmy Operations
Livy–Senior Consultant	Livy Consulting
Charlie–Sales Manager	Charlie Sales
Willy–Finance and Admin Manager	Willy Finance

I've structured the journey to success using the metaphor of the Galilean moons. The metaphor of the Fourth Moon provides a step-by-step guide to achieving optimal and sustainable success that any business can follow.

The First Moon is the moon of *strategy*. When you visit the First Moon, you develop your Strategic Plan. The Strategic Plan will be referred to as the Mission Plan.

The Second Moon is the moon of implementation. When you visit the Second Moon, you implement your Mission Plan.

The Third Moon is the moon of maintenance. When you visit the Third Moon, you commit to maintaining the strategy within your organization.

The Fourth Moon is the moon of leverage. It is the furthest moon and is only reached by a small percentage of businesses. If you reach the Fourth Moon, you will learn how to leverage true success within all aspects of your business and personal life. The Fourth Moon is the ultimate goal for any business owner, and offers extraordinary opportunities and riches.

Businesses that reach the Fourth Moon can expect to enjoy the following key benefits:

1. **Control and Confidence**—Run your business authentically, confident in the knowledge you can choose your own activities—whether business or personal.

2. **Fewer Hours**—Work less if you want.

3. **More Profit**—Earn higher profits.

4. **Reduced Stress**—Feel more relaxed.

5. **Lifestyle**—Create more options for yourself and your family with leverage.

6. **Refreshment and Reinvention**—Breathe new life into your daily routine and refine your life's purpose and meaning.

7. **Multiple Income Streams**—Expand your sources of income.

8. **Greater Wealth**—Increase personal net worth.

9. **Maximization of Business Value**—Receive higher-priced offers if you decide to sell your business.

10. **Succession Planning**—Develop a measured plan for your succession and execute it effectively.

But before you start . . .

As you venture on your initial journey, please don't jump around or rush ahead. Read through the book sequentially to understand the important role that each moon plays in contributing to your ultimate success.

Now let's go.

COMMITTING TO THE JOURNEY

Where the senses fail us, reason must step in.

—*Galileo Galilei*

CHAPTER 1

Houston, We Have a Problem

usiness has always fascinated me. I'm forever drawn to entrepreneurs, captivated by their stories and vision. Each story is unique.

I've worked with small and medium-sized businesses all my life. Drawing on my observations after working with hundreds of businesses, I have indulged my almost insatiable curiosity around the determinants of business success. Many observers get sidetracked by looking at the individual personalities of successful business owners. Of course, these personalities can differ dramatically and often don't illuminate the common, underlying themes of what made their business a success. I will focus here on these owners' disciplines, habits, and techniques within their businesses and in their personal lives.

Styles differ; but I'm interested in substance.

Despite differences in background, age, and even the industry of these successful leaders, the principles of success are amazingly consistent.

Using these time-tested and proven success strategies, I take my clients on a journey to the Fourth Moon. Not literally, of course, but the Fourth Moon metaphor illustrates how business owners can create sustainable success by visiting the four moons. Each moon represents a stage or milestone reached on this life-changing journey.

TOM DYLAN'S STORY BEGINS

Tom Dylan had been referred to me by Craig, a long-term client and friend.

Craig was genuinely concerned about Tom. He'd listened patiently to Tom talk about his business, Dylan IT, on many occasions over dinner and at social events. Craig respected Tom's expertise, and knew he had an established customer base; yet Tom always seemed out of control. His business life was full of drama. One crisis followed another. Despite this, Craig believed Tom had what it would take to reach the Fourth Moon.

Craig suggested that Tom begin to work with me. Tom was reluctant to "waste time," as he put it; but eventually he agreed to give me a call and set up an appointment.

Arriving at the offices of Dylan IT, I was promptly directed into Tom's office.

Tom's office was a mess. Paperwork, computer components, gadgets, and folders fought for space on his desk. A laptop computer and coffee mug had won the battle to the top of the pile.

Tom tore his attention from his laptop, looked up anxiously, and greeted me. "Oh, hi." He then looked back down to his computer.

"Hi," I said, standing in front of his desk. "I'm Darren Bourke. You called me for an appointment?"

Tom looked up again. "Of course, have a seat."

I could see that I would never get Tom's full attention, so I just jumped right in.

"To kick things off, Tom, why don't you tell me about Dylan IT?"

Tom ignored my question. He fiddled with his cell phone and glanced sideways at his open laptop, which was pinging loudly as each new email arrived.

"What did you say?"

"I said, why don't you tell me about Dylan IT?"

"Sorry, sorry. What do we do? We provide computer and IT support to businesses. This includes hardware, software, and consulting services with customers in various industries of all different sizes. I guess we try and meet all their needs as their external IT support partner."

Wow, I thought. That's a pretty broad offering.

"What about your team? Tell me about them," I continued, trying to keep him talking while he was focused.

"They're okay, I guess," he stammered. "There are twelve employees, excluding me. There are nine IT consultants. They tend to keep to themselves when they're in the office, but a lot of the time they're out at customers' offices. They seem productive, but it's hard to know because we constantly struggle to get them to complete timesheets, documentation, and invoices. Then there's Charlie, in Sales. We never know where Charlie is, or what he's up to. And finally there's Willy, who looks after Finance, with young Ella helping him in accounts."

Tom's assessment of his team wasn't glowing.

"What about your profitability and trading performance?" I said.

"It pays the bills," Tom calmly stated. "Look, I don't exactly know how much we make. I probably should know. We're always chasing outstanding accounts, and we don't always invoice customers for everything. It seems like so many things seem to get overlooked or stuck in this office."

I realized that Tom's world was less than perfect. He had an established business and loyal customers. But something was missing.

"Tell me, Tom, how do you—"

Before I could finish my question, a staff member burst into Tom's office unannounced. To my amazement, he launched into detailed discussions with Tom, seemingly oblivious to my presence. Worse still, Tom indulged him, and they spent more than five minutes talking while I sat agog. Tom shook his head, glanced at the mounting emails on his laptop, and scrolled through his phone. He appeared to be operating in a dazed and reactive state.

"How do you market and promote the business, Tom?" I continued, trying to get him back on track.

"Oh, the phone just rings. We have a paid advertisement in the business directory, and some customers refer others."

"And competitors?"

"There are a couple. The main one would be Peter Perfect. He is always sniffing around my customers and staff."

"Why do you call him Peter Perfect?"

"Peter's one of those guys who seems so perfect on the surface. He dresses immaculately, talks a big game, and charms people. But behind that façade there are some dodgy ethics. He hasn't been caught out yet, but he will be one day. That's for sure."

Tom's face had gone red and his blood pressure appeared to rise just by talking about his competitor.

"What about your profit margins?" I asked.

"We pay our staff and suppliers, and we did make a profit last year." Tom evaded the question impatiently.

"And how do you lead the team?" I asked, feeling I needed to change stride.

Tom leaned back in his chair proudly. "I try to lead the team. No one here does more hours than me."

"All right," I said, acknowledging Tom's pride in his work. "But who manages the team on an operational, day-to-day basis?"

"I do."

"It must be challenging to run internal meetings, deal with staff, meet prospects, and attend to management tasks in addition to spending significant hours on-site with customers."

This statement hung in the air for a few moments.

"Meetings are useless and overrated. Staff see me when they need to. I see customers every day, and the admin, well, it just has to wait. I'm too busy for all that," Tom stated firmly.

I'd asked enough questions to get a rough idea of the situation.

"I don't know about you, Tom, but I'm hungry. Why don't we duck out for a quick bite?"

"Now you're talking," Tom said with a wry grin, relaxing for the first time.

As we drove to a nearby restaurant, we chatted about personal matters. Tom was probably in his mid to late thirties. He would have been athletic in his youth, but looked as if he'd fallen into some poor dietary and lifestyle habits since starting the business. Tom was no poster boy for work-life balance.

On the surface, Tom seemed to have a good business. He'd been operating for a number of years and survived. He'd built a team around him from the early start-up days when it was just him, flying solo. He had a number of regular customers. While everything seemed rosy, there were serious issues lying beneath the surface.

We took our seats in the Italian restaurant.

"Forget all the business stuff for a moment," I said. "What about life away from the business?"

"It's not too bad, Darren. I suppose I don't see as much of my wife, Sarah, as I'd like to. I work long days—including some Saturdays—and she hates it when I open up the laptop on the couch in the evening. We never seem to take enough vacations because the business always needs me."

Tom went on to explain that his two kids were growing up way too quickly, and he was concerned his relationships with them were not as close as he desired. Sarah and Tom argued more often than in the past, he said; and with Tom's long work hours, they didn't spend much quality time together these days. Personal friendships had also lapsed due to Tom's demanding workload.

After a glass of wine, Tom confided that he was constantly stressed. He felt there was never enough time, and he had recurring thoughts that he wasn't successful. This endlessly played on his mind and affected his self-esteem.

As we finished our coffee, it was abundantly clear to me that Tom's business and personal life were far from optimal. He simply wasn't happy, and didn't enjoy the rewards and benefits that owning his own business should bring him.

While I'd managed to garner some initial insights about the business and about Tom's outlook, I was keen to get another perspective on the business: the staff's.

I asked him if it would be okay if I came back next week and met with his key people.

"That's fine," he said. "What do you want to speak to them about?"

"I want to get their thoughts and feedback on the business, and their roles within the company," I said, knowing this would reveal a great deal about Dylan IT. "Who are your key people?"

Tom explained there were four key employees. Of the nine IT consultants, he recommended I meet with Jimmy as the most senior consultant, and Livy as the next most senior. He also suggested I speak with Charlie about sales and Willy about the business's financial position.

So I asked Tom to speak with the four of them—Jimmy, Livy, Charlie, and Willy—about my upcoming visit. It was important that I see them separately and that they speak candidly. To get the most out of my discussions, I requested that Tom ask each of them to be open and honest in giving me feedback.

"You'll need to be open to constructive feedback yourself," I told him. "It's important if we're going to work together that we have the courage and commitment to tackle the real issues. Are you able to do that?"

Tom paused for a moment. "I guess I'll have to, if we're going to get any benefit out of you meeting up with them."

We scheduled some back-to-back times for me to meet the four key people—Jimmy, Livy, Charlie, and Willy—the following week.

Walking out of Tom's office, I was left to ponder the potential insights on the business through the eyes of the team. I sensed that Tom's cautiousness around me meeting the team was based on a fear of what they might say. Perhaps he felt vulnerable about their feedback validating his sense of low self-esteem and perceived lack of success.

Either way, my curiosity would be satisfied in a week's time. In the meantime, I'd keep an open mind.

CHAPTER 2

Discovery

As I sat patiently in the Dylan IT boardroom, I anticipated meeting Jimmy, Livy, Charlie, and Willy. It was important to get their feedback independent of Tom. I would then attempt to extract the challenges, frustrations, and opportunities the business faced, as well as those the team members faced individually.

Not wanting to be accused later of betraying their confidence, I explained that I would be sharing their feedback with Tom. As Tom was paying me to consult on business improvement, it was only fair and appropriate that I use their input for this purpose. I impressed upon them that their feedback would be used as constructive criticism only. No witch hunts would follow.

First up was Jimmy Operations, the most senior of Tom's IT consultants. After the usual introductions, we got down to business.

I began. "I'm keen to hear your perspective on the business, Jimmy, and in particular on your role in the company."

"Starting with the business, it has so much potential it's not funny. We are technically good at what we do, but we're always in chaos mode; we are reactive rather than proactive. Tom is so busy he finds it hard to manage the business. Customers bombard him with a heavy workload, and it hijacks him from us. As a result, we don't function well operationally. I hate to say it, but there's a real lack of communication. People tend to do their own thing, which hurts productivity. Lacking supervision, staff unfortunately make mistakes. Customers are regularly frustrated by our mistakes, and by consultants deferring scheduled visits because they've had to return to a previous job to fix a mistake. We just seem to be chasing our tails every day. I feel for Tom, because the business should be doing a lot better."

"Could you please expand on your IT team's operational work? What do they actually do, Jimmy?"

"We generally have projects where customers want hardware and software for their business. Our consultants provide advice on selecting the right solution, supply the hardware and software, and perform installation and training. We also offer IT support afterwards."

"And what about you, Jimmy, in relation to your own role?"

"I'm fairly independent, I guess. I try and help Tom out when he's not around with staff scheduling, customer relations, proposals, and invoicing. I work closely with Livy as well. I understand you're seeing her next. To be frank, my key frustration is a lack of access to Tom. Tom should delegate more. He can be a bit of a control freak. And we're so disorganized. I've suggested we should have regular meetings, but everyone's always too busy. I'm also worried that I'm not developing commercial and management skills like my peers in other companies."

Jimmy Operations expanded on the factors that were crippling the business. His honesty and genuine concern for Tom and the business were admirable. He was clearly talented, but I could see how frustrated and stressed he was by the environment at Dylan IT. Tom could lose him.

After finishing up with Jimmy, Livy Consulting joined me in the boardroom.

I could sense that she had plenty to say.

"I'm frustrated, Darren, by the lack of teamwork. Everyone acts independently. Jimmy and I try to help Tom manage the team better, but he's too busy and distracted with customer issues. We don't have an HR function in the business. Staff appraisals and pay reviews are never held, let alone training. As a result, overall staff morale is poor—though I hate to say it. I help Tom deal with staff issues when I have time, but I'd like the opportunity to develop some more formal management skills."

Livy Consulting shared similar frustrations to those shared by Jimmy. She, too, had been a loyal team member working hard in the trenches for Tom. I could see in Livy Consulting latent management talent. Her manner was relaxed but assertive. I could envision her supervising a team.

Charlie Sales looked after sales and marketing for the business and was next to join me.

"I don't know where to start, Darren. This business should do much more in sales revenue. Look, I don't know whether it's my fault or Tom's. I joined this business because I love sales and I'm interested in IT. I thought I could make a difference. But it's not working out. I need some direction, but Tom's always busy, and I can never get him to sit down and discuss our sales and marketing strategy. We don't have a plan. I don't have targets. Our pricing policy is unclear. I'm not even sure what our target market is. I've got to tell you, Darren, I'm really struggling."

As he talked, Charlie Sales became visibly emotional. I liked the fact that Charlie Sales cared. I could see his job satisfaction was at an all-time low. He was the Lone Ranger in sales and desperately needed guidance, structure, and support. Despite his emotional state, I could see the magnetic traits of a successful salesman in Charlie Sales.

The last of the key team members to join me was Willy Finance. Willy was responsible for the finance and administration of the business.

"How would you assess the finance area of the business, Willy?" I asked.

"That's a loaded question," Willy said, flashing a nervous smile. "I'd like to say it was in excellent health, but that wouldn't be accurate. Let's just say that Finance and Tom aren't the best of friends. It is impossible to get Tom to look at the figures. I need to sit down with him each week to go through the numbers, but he's never available. As a result, cash flow is constantly a problem. Because Tom doesn't complete timesheets, the consultants get away with incomplete or late time recording. I'd hate to think how much money the business loses as a result of chargeable time not being recorded or billed. Poor Ella in accounts is constantly chasing timesheets so we can invoice."

Willy Finance's frustrations were valid. He had to deal with Tom venting about cash-flow issues. He also had to take the angry phone calls from customers who received unexpected invoices, and from suppliers chasing unpaid accounts. After calming down a little, Willy Finance went on to explain his desire to help the business grow and to be more commercially involved in the business.

It had been a solid couple of hours spent with the Dylan IT team. Jimmy Operations, Livy Consulting, Charlie Sales, and Willy Finance had provided important insights, which I combined with what I'd learned from Tom during our initial meeting. There was an underlying correlation among everyone's feedback: the business, the key team members, and Tom were all under huge stress; they felt dissatisfied and unrewarded. Operationally, the business was dysfunctional. It was only a matter of time before key team members would break down, and customers would start leaving the business. The future of the business was at risk.

There was no time for timidity or half-truths. I walked into Tom's office and told him that I had completed my discussions with Jimmy Operations, Livy Consulting, Charlie Sales, and Willy Finance. I further explained that I needed to share their feedback and discuss the implications with him while it was fresh in my mind. He agreed. Keen to speak privately, and the morning now behind us, Tom suggested we head off-site for lunch.

Sitting down to lunch, we got straight down to it.

I implored Tom to view the feedback as constructive rather than critical. Owners generally become defensive when confronted with feedback about them individually and about their business. It is human nature for such feedback to go straight to the heart. In my work over the years, I'd observed owners who refused to accept or reflect on feedback from their team or their customers. Where the feedback was valid, this response almost always resulted in the business either closing or facing a long and sustained period of mediocrity.

After getting Tom's assurances that he would take on the team's feedback constructively, I set about sharing the thoughts of Jimmy Operations, Livy Consulting, Charlie Sales, and Willy Finance.

I spoke quietly and slowly. I first took Tom through Jimmy Operations's frustrations in being unable to access Tom. I recounted Jimmy's observations on operational dysfunction, lack of delegation, and overall chaos surrounding the business.

Livy Consulting's observations, I explained, were more focused on personnel. Livy was frustrated by the lack of systems, support, and general management around staff. As a result, overall staff performance and morale—in Livy's opinion—were poor.

I paused momentarily to allow Tom to take in this first dose of feedback.

Charlie Sales felt terrible about Dylan IT's sales performance, and suggested it could be significantly improved. Charlie longed for a clear sales and marketing strategy. He desperately sought clarity on sales targets and pricing policy, and he was racked with self-doubt around his own ability.

I told Tom about Willy Finance's frustrations in having to deal with constant cash-flow problems. The lack of systems and poor time-recording practices made running the finance and admin side of the business a living nightmare.

Tom tried to constructively process these fresh, yet painful, insights. I could see that it was hard for him. No matter how hard he tried to stay objective, the feedback struck him as personal criticism.

"I must say, Tom, that the sessions I held with Jimmy, Livy, Charlie, and Willy all had the same underlying theme," I said.

"Yeah, I'm sure they did," said Tom. "They all said the business sucks, and it's my fault. I can't believe that I've been so delusional in running the business. I feel like a fool. They must really hate me, don't they?"

"Quite the contrary," I said, and paused. "What I meant about the underlying theme in all four sessions was how much they actually *care* about you and the business."

"Really?" said Tom, lifting his head.

I recounted to Tom the hundreds of team members I'd spoken to individually over many years, and explained the various stages of feelings these team members are likely to go through. First comes frustration. It can be mild or acute. Second comes disengagement. This is where employees reach the conclusion that they can't change or fix things. They just feel numb. Third come anger and shutdown. This stage can be dangerous, because anger brings volatility, and shutdown represents mental resignation. Team members in shutdown mode may lack care and accountability for their role, without the owner realizing what's happened. The fourth and final stage is a meltdown or breakdown. Short of a dramatic meltdown, the employee might simply resign without warning.

"So I could lose the team?" Tom suggested.

"Well, yes, you could if you take no action, Tom. But what I said before about how much they cared, I really meant it. The good news is that Jimmy Operations, Livy Consulting, Charlie Sales, and Willy Finance are in the early stages, feeling somewhere between frustration and disengagement. If you address this now, you can stop these feelings of frustration and disengagement from accelerating into anger, or meltdown, and prevent your key people from resigning."

I wanted to share with Tom some feelings expressed by the team in order to balance their operational feedback.

"Jimmy Operations genuinely feels for you. He expressed concern about the business not performing well for you. His tone was more caring than critical. I honestly believe he cares for the business. He wants to do more to help, but he feels surrounded by chaos.

"Livy Consulting feels for the staff. She wants to help you develop and implement personnel systems around the team. No doubt she possesses the people skills to assist here.

"Charlie Sales was emotional about the sales revenue of the business. With a lack of sales strategy and limited access to you, he feels alone and incompetent. But I saw some attributes in Charlie that we can work with.

"Willy Finance feels the brunt of the operational dysfunction. Remember, he takes the angry calls from suppliers chasing payments. He takes the phone calls from frustrated customers complaining about their fees. Willy has to juggle cash flow, deal with your emotional outbursts, and try to keep the business afloat. It's a tough gig. Willy desperately seeks organizational structure.

"And what they all want is to help build a great business. They all recognize they have a role to play. They need access to you. They need procedures, systems, and strategies to create rhythm within the business operationally. Jimmy, Livy, and Willy want to develop their management skills—skills that their peers are currently developing in other organizations."

"I see," Tom said. "I can understand how they must feel. If I'm to be completely honest, I've seen this coming. I just haven't wanted to. I've had neither the capacity nor the courage to face it. By keeping myself so distracted with hands-on work, I've been able to hide from the spotlight. Sometimes it takes confronting feedback to finally acknowledge the reality of things."

Tom's acknowledgment and acceptance of the team's feedback was an epiphany for him. I wanted him to remember this watershed moment. It could be the potential starting point for his transformative journey to the Fourth Moon.

I introduced Galileo's story to Tom, and explained the way he approached his search with patience, open-mindedness, and perseverance. If Tom was to turn around not only the business's fortunes but also his personal life, he, too, would have to adopt these attitudes.

Tom was rather confused at first. I could see him wondering, "What does Galileo have to do with my business?" But as he listened, he became curious, especially when I related the astronomer's patience, open-mindedness, and perseverance to Tom's situation at Dylan IT.

I told Tom that he had already demonstrated an open mind in accepting the observations and feedback from his team. An open mind would still be needed in the future, as the team's feedback was just the tip of the iceberg. Customers, suppliers, his wife, Sarah, and even Tom himself would surely have further insights.

Patience was an attribute Tom would have to adopt from Galileo. Tom's nature was reactive rather than proactive, chaotic rather than planned, sporadic rather than sustained. Tom would surely have to become more patient if his life was going to change dramatically.

Perseverance was not foreign to Tom. He had survived infancy in his business, and had already beaten the odds. He had the work ethic of a diamond miner. However, a new perseverance was required now. The perseverance to play a new game, committed to the actions and disciplines required to create sustainable success.

Tom acknowledged Galileo's attitudes and considered how he could adopt these more successfully in the future. Today's epiphany was still fresh on his mind, although he clearly held some self-doubts around his ability to dig himself out of the cavernous hole he currently found himself in.

I wanted to introduce the story of Galileo's discovery of the four moons of Jupiter to get Tom thinking before my next visit. I recounted the patience, open-mindedness, and perseverance required in order for the astronomer to gaze intently for hours into the night sky.

Tom listened carefully as I spoke of that night in 1610 when Galileo first observed the moons, just before discovering that they orbited Jupiter. In these moments, Galileo disposed of centuries' of belief in the theory that all heavenly bodies circled Earth. Tom needed a similar revolution in the way he viewed his business.

"I want to talk to you more about these moons next time we meet," I proposed to Tom. "But first I want you to reflect on something. What if I told you that I take clients on a journey to these four moons? Not literally of course, but in a metaphorical sense in which each moon represents a stage or milestone in their journey toward sustainable business success. Curious?"

"Assuming you haven't lost your marbles, it sounds interesting," Tom laughed.

"I haven't been certified yet, Tom!" I joked. "Before we catch up next, I want you to think deeply about the feedback you received today from your team, and about our searching discussions that followed. I want you to think about what you really want to achieve in business and in life. Challenge yourself to consider committing to a journey beyond today's insights. Think about Galileo's open-mindedness, and about his patience and perseverance. You, and only you, can decide if you're up for the challenge of making significant and sustained changes in your life."

Tom would head home tonight full of thoughts, questions, and perhaps some regrets. Sleep would elude him as his mind raced through opportunities, fears, and potential resolutions.

PRE-MISSION PLANNING

We cannot teach people anything;
we can only help them discover it within themselves.

—Galileo Galilei

CHAPTER 3

The Four Moons: The Journey Ahead

Following his recent discoveries, I'd intentionally left Tom to ponder the prospect of embarking on a journey.

Having heard the metaphor of the four moons of Jupiter, Tom accepted my invitation to indulge me in expanding on this. I promised him that it would all tie back to a key decision he would need to make about Dylan IT and ultimately his future.

I introduced Tom to the names of the four moons:

* Io
* Europa
* Ganymede
* Callisto

"Ready to take a metaphorical walk around the four moons?" I asked.

"I've got my space suit on," Tom chuckled.

THE FIRST MOON: STRATEGY

Io, the First Moon of Jupiter, is the fourth largest moon in the solar system. Described as "the pizza moon," it has over 400 active volcanoes that paint the surface in numerous shades of yellow, red, white, black, and green.

Io is the most geologically active object in the solar system, as Io's interior is pulled between Jupiter and the other three Galilean moons.

"Imagine landing on the First Moon," I said. "It immediately hits you how large Io, the moon of strategy, actually is. Strategy is vast, and it's the foundation of our vision.

"It is fitting that Io is the most geologically active object in the solar system, because our strategy is what pulls us between the other three moons of implementation, maintenance, and leverage.

"It is also convenient that Io is so large, since we will need to easily find it as we regularly return to change, modify, and tweak our strategy."

Watching Tom's face, I could see that he realized he had never journeyed to the First Moon. He hadn't taken the time to devise and document a strategy. Tom had not set the coordinates for his success. Business and life occurred on an ad hoc basis with no structure, plan, or direction.

"Io is your first destination, and I can take you there," I said with encouragement. "On Io, we can stop all the noise, stop the distractions, and develop your strategy. Imagine sitting down and reflecting on how you would like to set up your business life and personal life. Together we will develop a plan for the future, a plan you can carry forward on your journey to the other moons. Not only that, but on Io we document your strategy so that it is written down to review and measure progress against. It can be shown to your key team members and discussed with stakeholders so that we are all pulling in the same direction."

Tom nodded and sat more relaxed as he considered the resources on Io. He also reminded himself that he would not be alone there.

Having introduced the moon Io—strategy—I moved on to the Second Moon, Europa.

THE SECOND MOON: IMPLEMENTATION

Europa, the Second Moon of Jupiter, is small and is the smoothest object in our solar system. It is thought to have twice the water volume of Earth.

The small size of Europa—implementation—is quite appropriate. Business owners think that implementation on Europa is a small thing. A minor detail. They believe that talking about their strategy is the same as implementing it. But knowing isn't doing. Great things have to be actioned—have to be implemented. Winners implement.

"Like Europa, the implementation of your strategy needs to be fluid and smooth," I said. "Implementation may not work or 'stick' on the first few attempts. You and your team must be fluid in your approach to implementing strategy. Trial and error may be required in getting the processes, procedures, and resources in the right order and flowing correctly to deliver predictable outcomes. Once implementation is in place, rolling out strategy becomes smooth and streamlined. Of course there will be hiccups and obstacles, but the ability to return back to the implementation stage navigates the ship back on course."

"Okay," said Tom. "I'm liking this. Smooth and fluid implementation of my strategy. Just like Europa's surface."

"You've got it, Tom. So to recap: Reaching the First Moon, Io, we develop and document your strategy. We travel on to arrive at Europa, where we adopt a fluid approach to implementing your strategy smoothly. Then, and only then, can we continue our journey to the Third Moon, Ganymede—the moon of maintenance."

THE THIRD MOON: MAINTENANCE

Ganymede, the Third Moon of Jupiter, is the largest moon in the solar system. In fact, Ganymede is even visible with the naked eye. Its surface can be divided into two types of terrain—dark and light.

"It's good that Ganymede is so visible. Of the businesses that might reach the Third Moon, most owners and teams waste their time on the Third Moon and actually cheat."

"What do you mean they cheat?" Tom asked.

"They don't actually maintain their strategy, having developed it on the First Moon and implemented it on the Second Moon. All that work, yet they don't honor their strategy by maintaining it. Third Moon activity is about working on maintaining the commitment to key priorities, agreed actions, disciplines, and procedures. The dark and light terrain of Ganymede highlights the contrast between cheating (dark) and maintenance (light). It's not difficult to establish who is honoring maintenance of strategy on the Third Moon. And remember that only visitors occupying the light terrain get to continue their journey on to the Fourth Moon."

Tom was keeping up with my metaphor and seemed to be enjoying it.

THE FOURTH MOON: LEVERAGE

Callisto, the Fourth Moon, has an ancient crust dating back some four billion years. Callisto has a thin atmosphere of carbon dioxide. Scientists believe the atmosphere is constantly replenished by the slow sublimation of carbon dioxide ice.

"Businesses that reach the Fourth Moon enjoy leverage," I said. "Leverage is all about having additional capacity in your life. Financial freedom, predictable business performance, and an abundance of time allocated to activities of choice make Callisto a business and personal nirvana.

"The ancient crust represents establishment and maturity. Like the ancient icons we worship on earth, visitors to the Fourth Moon respect their presence and time on Callisto. It is lightly populated, and all its visitors have earned their place on the planet.

"Callisto's replenishment of its atmosphere can be compared to the independent successful business owner. With a proven and established model for success, the business owner that reaches the Fourth Moon can replenish his or her reserves. Reliant on no one, they have the self-sufficiency to have total freedom in their life choices."

Tom was leaning forward listening intently; his relaxed face and his body language told me he was enchanted with the idea of landing on Callisto.

"Explaining the journey as a story has made everything so much clearer," Tom said. "I know I'm not in the best place right now, and I'm sure I need your help to get me to the Fourth Moon, but I feel really strongly about taking the journey now."

"You don't want to sleep on it and take a few days to consider if you are up for the challenge?" I offered.

"No. I'm in," Tom stated emphatically. "How do we start?"

"We need to do a flight check before we leave the ground. I'd like to meet next to talk about some high-level strategy. I want to challenge you more specifically on what you want to achieve over the medium to long term in reaching the Fourth Moon. We've got to talk about a few home truths and take a reality check, just to make sure we're ready to commence the journey. Once we take off, we don't want to be aborting the mission."

Tom and I wound up our session together with Tom committed to reflecting on his big-picture strategy before our next meeting. It had been a great day and somewhat of a breakthrough. The metaphor of the four moons had piqued Tom's interest and crystallized his desire.

He had now made the commitment to taking the journey. It was his decision without being forced, cajoled, or falsely convinced. He was empowered and engaged. Tom was finally ready to get onboard.

CHAPTER 4

Flight Check:
Before We Leave the Ground

The knock on my car window startled me. It was Tom.

Having just parked my car in the Dylan IT parking lot, I gazed out my window to see Tom standing straight, arms by his side, with a beaming grin on his face. I momentarily imagined him as an astronaut reporting for duty.

After the usual pleasantries, we walked inside Tom's building together and entered the boardroom.

"I wanted to run a flight check today, Tom. It's worthwhile going over the journey ahead to manage your expectations before we leave the ground. I also need some big-picture thinking from you on your strategy, goals, and desires to help set some coordinates. No point having a GPS if we don't know the destination."

"Fire away, Darren."

"From a business perspective, I want you to comment on the desired size of the business, ideal sales revenues, and operating profitability. What markets do you want to trade in—both from a product and service perspective, as well as geographically? I want you to think deeply about your purpose and what the endgame might look like. Do you want to work in the business forever, or do you envisage hiring an Operations Manager so that you can transition to a nonexecutive role? Do you want to grow the business and sell it to a competitor? You might want to pass it on to your children or set up a staged management buyout for your team to succeed you. You should think about these things long and hard, but for now, I want you to consider your long-term goals and objectives."

"It's hard to think years ahead, given my current head-space," Tom said. "I understand I need to think more strategically over different timeframes, but having never done it, it's a bit overwhelming."

"That's totally understandable, Tom. It's the same for every business owner facing this for the first time. Just start by thinking out loud about what Dylan IT might look like in ten years if it was really successful. Let's try and come up with five big things. Don't hold back. Really think big."

"Well, I love my work, so I'd like to continue as a consultant to my favorite customers, and it would be great to have a management team."

"Great. Keep going, Tom."

"I realize now that I haven't been rewarded as much as I'd like for my efforts. I want to create wealth and financial independence for Sarah, the kids, and me. I guess I'd also hope to be more of a leader in my field. With all this planning, I probably should have a Succession Plan in place by then, too. I've always thought it would be good one day to sell part of the business to the key people who built it with me, so that's an option."

"Wow, Tom. You have been thinking about this since our last meeting. You've really nailed that. Let me recap on this while it's fresh and top-of-mind."

Here's what I noted down for Tom's long-term strategy:

1. Consult to favorite customers and support an internal management team.

2. Create wealth and financial independence.

3. Be a market leader in field.

4. Have a clear and documented Succession Plan.

5. Consider potential management buyout.

"Now let's shift your focus to the medium term, Tom. Let's look at three to five years from now. What are your thoughts?"

"I'd want the business to have a strong General Manager or Operations Manager to run the business day to day," Tom said. "I would like the business to specialize more. We've got to improve productivity and reduce my hands-on role. So the need to build a performing team is critical. Another thing I've always wanted to do is systematize our business processes. We are really weak in that area. And finally, marketing and sales needs to become a major focus if I'm ever going to get rich."

"I just wrote these down as you were speaking. Are these right?" I asked.

Tom's medium-term goals:

1. To have a strong Operations Manager to run operations.
2. To specialize more.
3. To build an established and productive team with less reliance on Tom as key man.
4. To put systematized business processes in place.
5. To focus marketing and sales to deliver higher revenue.

Tom nodded.

I let Tom have a break from brainstorming and turned to introducing the role his team could play in making these goals happen.

"Before we take off, we will need to get the team to support us, Tom. Let's think about what each team member can contribute. We also need to be mindful of the insights I gathered in my individual meetings with Jimmy Operations, Livy Consulting, Charlie Sales, and Willy Finance. The trick is to get synergy working within Dylan IT. If the contribution you need from team members marries up with their needs and wants, and their contribution directly aids the achievement of your goals, you've got it made."

"Can you expand on this using individual team members?" Tom asked curiously.

"Absolutely, Tom. Let's do it now. Jimmy Operations wants to develop his commercial and management skills. You want an Operations Manager, a second-in-charge, to run operations. If you let go, and empower Jimmy to transition into running the business over time, he develops his skills, Dylan IT has an Operations Manager, and you start getting your life back."

"Okay, that's a huge payoff. What about Livy?" Tom said.

"Livy Consulting wants to develop the team and grow her personnel management skills. You want to build an established, productive team with less reliance on you. Again, if you support Livy in managing the consulting team, you could both achieve what you want."

Tom smiled. "Synergy at work again. Now what about Charlie?"

"Charlie Sales wants to grow the business. He needs access to you and desperately wants a plan around sales and marketing. With Jimmy Operations and Livy Consulting stepping up, you should have more time to develop the marketing, sales, and communication model for Dylan IT. Charlie can even help you develop a specialization for the business. This could grow revenue and increase profitability.

"And of course," I continued, "Willy Finance can be the glue that holds it all together. With more time available operationally, you can schedule time with Willy. And doesn't he need it? It's your business, Tom, so you need to start understanding the numbers, the cash flow, and the profitability. With access to you and a feeling of empowerment, Willy could start to work on systematizing the business processes of Dylan IT."

"What an opportunity!" Tom said. "I can see so clearly how my goals and dreams can include the team's wants and needs. This can be win-win for all of us. But how do we make this happen with the team?"

"That's an important question, Tom, and one that must be handled deftly over the entire journey. I'm not going to confuse you at this stage with too much detail, but I will tell you this: I want you to do two things on this, following our meeting today."

"What are the two things?" Tom asked.

"First, I want you to meet with Jimmy Operations, Livy Consulting, Charlie Sales, and Willy Finance all together as a group. At this group meeting, I want you to share your discovery and speak openly about the journey ahead that you've committed to. Keep it big picture, and from the heart. Second, explain to them that following this group meeting, you'll be scheduling individual meetings with each of them to explain their role on the journey—the mission—and what they'll get out of it. Tell them that we will get more input from them when we are developing our strategy after takeoff. On the First Moon, Io, we will be developing and documenting the Dylan IT strategy. That will be enough for now."

"All right, so that's the team involvement. What should I expect over the journey?" Tom asked.

"It's important to manage your expectations here," I said. "There are no quick fixes or shortcuts here, as I've said before. It will take time. Some businesses, if they really push and everything goes well, might reach the Fourth Moon in just two short years. But for most that get there, it can take three to five years. Remember, most don't make it to the Fourth Moon, ever.

"There are also costs, both financial and personal. There are obviously the financial costs required to fix and optimize the business. And then there are the personal costs of letting go, empowering others, embracing change, and the humility required to admit past failures."

Tom was listening intently and motioned for me to continue.

"I ask that you now begin getting stakeholders onboard with your Mission Plan. Not too transparently, but start thinking about communicating differently with them."

"Mission Plan?" Tom queried.

"The Mission Plan is what we'll call your Strategic Plan. Your strategy."

"And who are the stakeholders you refer to?"

"There are four key stakeholder groups: customers, employees, shareholders, and suppliers. They all have different profiles, have different needs, and play different roles in influencing whether you reach the Fourth Moon. Let's call this the Stakeholder Quadrant. We will investigate this quadrant in more detail when you reach the Third Moon of maintenance—Ganymede.

"But in the meantime, I propose this: get closer to your customers, listen to their feedback, and analyze where each customer sits within your future plans. Build deeper relationships with your key employees through goal setting for mutual benefit. Include Sarah as a shareholder in explaining your plans and how this will improve your lives. And finally, see your suppliers as an integral part of your business. How can you build stronger relationships that create a competitive advantage for Dylan IT while rewarding suppliers with your loyalty? All these four stakeholder relationships can be nurtured, developed, and worked on from this moment forward. I offer that challenge to you, Tom."

"I feel like I need to protect myself from myself," Tom confessed. "When I'm talking with you I feel motivated and confident, but that little voice in my head can be negative. I'm conscious that being a control freak, I will slip back into bad habits. I don't want to keep doing horrendous hours for little reward. I deserve better. Sarah and the kids deserve better. I need you to remind me if I slip back, and to call me out on it," Tom pleaded.

"Just on that, Tom, let me tell you the story of the work paradigm and the Busy Fool. Let's make a pledge now that we'll call out the Busy Fool if we see him. Let me explain."

THE PARABLE OF THE BUSY FOOL

"The Busy Fool keeps himself constantly busy so he never has to see who he really is. The Busy Fool spends years toiling away. He doesn't have to think, plan, or develop a strategy. He just works. He doesn't truly help others, foster relationships, or invest in other people. He is an island. An island that never stops working. He can't be queried, challenged, or attacked for his autocratic style, his grumpy demeanor, or his emotionless state. It would be like attacking Mother Teresa. How can you attack someone that works so hard and so selflessly? What a man.

"But one day the Busy Fool loses his business, gets sick, or has to retire. The Busy Fool returns home to his empty house. His second wife left him. His kids know him only as a stranger. He doesn't have any real friends because he is always working. Worse still, he doesn't have any hobbies and interests, as these were never developed during his forty years of work. But, the Busy Fool argues, he has a pile of money so high that one couldn't jump over it—or spend it—in a lifetime.

"Unfortunately, the Busy Fool has no family to share this pile of money with, no friends to spend it with, nor hobbies or interests to spend it on. So sad. Just eighteen months after stopping work, the Busy Fool dies as an unhealthy, lonely man. At his funeral, attended largely by business acquaintances, the priest delivers the eulogy, with no family or friends available to speak. The priest says he worked hard and was wealthy. No one cries. The coffin is carried out. The end.

"Is that how we want to live our lives and to be remembered?" I asked. "There are Busy Fools everywhere. You just don't want to become one. The Busy Fool works under the man-made work paradigm. The work paradigm is the conventional belief that everyone must work 9 to 5, Monday to Friday, nearly every week, in every year until they are very old. It's a strange paradigm. Five days out of seven, nearly every week for the foreseeable future. With human nature's materialism and desire for status—especially in Western culture—combined with the constantly plugged-in technology age, the work paradigm has extended from 9 AM to 5 PM, to 8 AM to 6 PM, and now 7 AM to 7 PM and beyond. Twelve-hour days are the norm now in many workplaces.

"What the Busy Fool and many employees don't understand is that the new world economy is about output, not hours. Get in, do what you need to do, and get out. Make it happen. For yourself, your life," I said.

"I think I know what that guy looks like," Tom said. "I see him in the mirror shaving each morning."

Tom's humility and humor were perfect for the moment, and we both broke out laughing.

"Now the final thing I want to do before we leave the ground and commence your journey is to revisit Galileo's three attitudes. Do you remember them, Tom?" I asked.

"Patience, open-mindedness, and perseverance," he said.

"And you will need to carry these attitudes in your pocket over the entire journey," I suggested.

"These three attitudes will be needed on each moon as you challenge yourself and the team to adopt new beliefs, habits, and behaviors required to reach the Fourth Moon. But I know you can do it, Tom. I've seen a shift in you."

"I'm ready, Darren."

"Next time we catch up we'll be taking off to explore Io, strategy, so I want you to think about the year ahead and what you want to achieve. The short-term objectives, of course, lead to achieving the medium- and long-term objectives. Our progress is sequential. We must go one moon at a time.

"Don't forget to follow up on meeting Jimmy Operations, Livy Consulting, Charlie Sales, and Willy Finance together as a group and individually."

Tom assured me he'd schedule those meetings with the team, and that he'd be ready to kick off the mission.

Driving home from our meeting, I cast my mind forward to the First Moon of Io. Io's size and volcanic activity would no doubt challenge Tom and his team. However, Tom had demonstrated some mettle today, and we couldn't be more prepared for takeoff.

The First Moon of strategy awaited.

THE FIRST MOON:
STRATEGY

All truths are easy to understand once they are discovered;
the point is to discover them.

—Galileo Galilei

CHAPTER 5

Exploring Io:
Developing Strategy

Tom had requested to meet away from the Dylan IT offices for his maiden journey to the First Moon of Io.

We'd chosen a historic boathouse with an outdoor café overlooking a river. The air was crisp and the sky clear, with native birds enjoying the sanctuary of the riverbank. It was an ideal location for First Moon thinking on strategy.

"It's time to put on our space suits," I suggested to Tom, "to explore the First Moon."

But Tom resisted. "Already?"

"You've been waiting for this journey to begin," I said. "It begins right now, here on Io—the First Moon. We aren't in a conference room anymore. We are on the First Moon, Io, strategy. Io is large and active. Imagine that you can hear the active volcanoes on Io. They aren't deafening, but rather rhythmic, as they seem to breathe and sigh.

"The geological activity of Io is powerful. We will use Io's activity to act as a force to propel us on to the other moons.

"It's time to develop your Strategic Plan, Tom. Or what we'll refer to from now on as your Mission Plan," I announced as our lattes arrived.

I was trying to facilitate a creative, fun, and fluid environment on the First Moon, quite intentionally. Development of a winning strategy involves lateral thinking. That is, solving complex problems by thinking outside the box.

I explained to Tom that it was critical that the Mission Plan be truly owned by him. As founder and owner of Dylan IT, he needed to believe in the plan and be accountable for delivering on it. Tom's team also needed to understand the business strategy and how it related to their roles.

"How did it go in your meetings with the management team as a group and individually?"

"Really well, actually," Tom replied. "The team meeting was a good chance to talk to everyone together. They appeared to appreciate a commitment to change, and to doing things a different way. I was pretty frank and humble about my recent discoveries, and about the impact my habits and behavior have had on the business."

"And the individual catch-ups. How did they go?"

"Well, that's where it got really interesting. Jimmy Operations, Livy Consulting, Charlie Sales, and Willy Finance all got pretty fired up."

"How so?"

"In a good way. Each in their individual style, and in their own words, they suggested that they wanted to be part of something bigger and better. Each one of them shared similar observations to those they shared with you. Being prepared for this from your earlier feedback helped. It was actually quite inspiring. I believe they really do want to contribute, to help. But I understand now that I need to deliver them something from this journey beyond their salaries."

"That's great, Tom," I said. "That's what I'd hoped to hear. Did you tell them that we'd be meeting with them again soon to discuss the business strategy for Dylan IT and their specific roles in relation to this strategy?"

"Yes. I assured them they'd be involved in things more regularly moving forward," Tom confirmed.

I reminded Tom of our last brainstorming session where we'd listed his medium- and long-term goals. It was now time to set up the short-term goals, priorities, and targets for the year ahead.

"To develop and document your strategy for the financial year ahead, we'll need to establish a calendar, scoreboard, and reporting system to drive and measure the achievement of your goals. I recommend you follow a technique used by successful entrepreneurs. They write their top five goals on small flash cards and carry them in their pockets to remind themselves what to focus on. If you're not working on your top five goals most of your working week, you simply won't reach the Fourth Moon."

"Why should I bother to write a list?" Tom queried. "I can keep what's important in my head."

"Tom, we are trained from a young age to be constant list makers. There is merit in this, and it serves us well. Constant, detailed note-taking through shopping lists, jobs to do at home, and other lists are effective in capturing everything and missing nothing. But running a successful business is not about including everything. Business owners are 'time poor'—there's not enough time for everything they need to do, what with so many competing priorities. It's about knowing what is most important and getting that done. Focusing on these top five goals helps us to prioritize our tasks."

Tom quizzed me on what areas successful businesses typically focus on when setting their top five goals. I explained that despite the industry or size of business, top priorities were amazingly similar. Of all the key goals observed, the majority covered areas such as growth, profitability, productivity, personnel, products and services, sales, marketing, management, customers, wealth creation, succession, and systems.

"Why should I limit myself to only five goals?" Tom asked.

"In limiting your goals to five, you put subconscious pressure on yourself to address them. As an entrepreneur, you will always have new ideas and goals that you want to add to your list. But the rule is that you can't add a new goal to your list until a spot becomes free. Internal psychology goes to work in getting that new goal into your top five. This technique alone will provide a critical and defining shift for you as a business owner.

"Old habits die hard, and there is a lot of conditioning to unwind. To many businesspeople, this need to limit key priorities to a list of just five may sound counterintuitive. That's not to say you stop noting down ideas and attending to the never-ending list of tasks and actions. It just means you shift responsibility and the allocation of time spent on these tasks.

"Now, after you come up with your top five goals, you need a sentence or two to describe what needs to be done. After concisely describing each goal, you then need to select an Internal Champion."

"An Internal Champion?"

"The Internal Champion is accountable for the goal. This could be you, a member of your team, or an external party. Finally, notice that there is a deadline set to ensure the goal is completed. The mechanism of this simple structure works extremely efficiently. With an Internal Champion accountable for the goal, your team is never confused or ignorant about who actually owns the task. You avoid the pitfalls of circular discussion in meetings, time decay, or other operational black spots where priorities die. There is nowhere to run, nowhere to hide."

I explained that with an Internal Champion, the owner and senior management team now have greater leverage in their roles. The management team can get involved regularly, but it need be only for short periods of time, to help the Internal Champion achieve the goal. Short, sharp meetings or "check-ins" during day-to-day operations help the Internal Champions to progress by answering questions, bringing in internal or external help, or contacting other parties to move forward on those goals. This support mechanism not only helps achieve the goal, but also empowers the Internal Champion to complete tasks against the working deadline. The monitoring of the goals in this way drives implementation.

"The Internal Champion accountable for delivering on the goal will be selected from Jimmy Operations, Livy Consulting, Charlie Sales, Willy Finance, and of course you, Tom."

I explained to Tom that Jimmy, Livy, Charlie, Willy, and Tom himself were all free to ask the Internal Champion the status of the goal without having to tiptoe around the issue. The team is there to assist the Internal Champion with completing the goal by helping to remove barriers and obstacles. Productivity improves as other team members are not distracted by goals they're not accountable for.

"Later we'll go through how to set goals for each individual team member. These are ultimately linked to the business's goals."

By capping his critical priorities to five, Tom could focus most of his energy on these important areas. A new priority could only be taken up if one of the existing priorities were "done" or "dropped."

A goal is "done" when it is implemented and completed. While this may seem self-explanatory, it isn't always. The business must drive a culture of completeness. A goal is not done until it is alive within the organization. The marketing brochure is not done until there are copies printed, stored for easy access, distributed to team members, and given out to sales prospects. There can be no wiggle room for "done." It is either done, or not done.

"Drop" your goal when circumstances change. There are many instances when a past goal is no longer a priority to you. Acquisition of a major customer may have been a goal until that prospect joined a competitor. A potential new division of the business, formerly considered a great idea, may no longer hold appeal after some due diligence work is completed. Don't hold on to a goal that no longer holds appeal or relevancy just because it used to. It's like feeding a dead goldfish. If it's gone, drop it and let a new, emerging goal get on your top five list.

In limiting your goals to five, and allowing only new goals to come to life when the existing goals are done or dropped, you create a natural vacuum that forces you to implement and execute with a laser-like precision throughout the organization.

The management team should spend the majority of their time driving the goals to completion, either directly or indirectly, by supporting the Internal Champions.

TARGETS

"No Mission Plan is complete," I continued, "without setting up sales targets and budgets for the future. I recommend you start by focusing on sales revenue, cost of sales, gross profit, general overhead expenditure, and net operating profit. These targets, both in dollars and percentages, should be known like family.

"Other additional targets or key performance indicators can be developed over time and included in future plans. These may include number of active customers, number of transactions, average transaction value, average cost to produce, and other ratios and measures.

"I will expand on finance and reporting when we get to the Third Moon. The important thing, Tom, is that you have to own the Mission Plan. You must believe in it because you are ultimately accountable for delivering it.

You are the one who has to communicate to your team the business's strategy and how that strategy relates to their roles."

DOCUMENTATION

"If it's not written down, it's not real. Simple as that. You need to write down your plan—ideally on one page.

"Regardless of the template or format used, you should aim for one page. My preference is to use an Excel spreadsheet format, and enlarge it for ease of reading.

"I also recommend you create two versions. The second one should be a slightly modified version for a wider audience. I call these two versions private and public. The private version contains all information, warts and all, showing bottom-line profitability and other sensitive information. This is generally used by owners. The public version is simply the private version with any sensitive information taken out. For example, you may not want to share your operating profit with your management team. Some people may, but I've found that most don't.

"I know we workshopped your medium- and long-term goals in our pre-mission planning, but I want to come back now to you defining your top five goals for the financial year ahead. We can put the required detail around these later, but for now let's get these down."

"First things first," Tom said. "I've never had a strategy, so I'd better document it and implement it with the team. Then I want to do a full review of our services, products, and pricing. Of course, our staff structure needs a review. I've realized we're too reliant on me, so some major work on management and operating systems is needed. Then the marketing and sales stuff has to be bolted on to the other primary goals to connect it to our customers and market."

Tom and I then discussed the selection of Internal Champions as a goal for the business. It was tempting to make Tom the Internal Champion for each goal, given that the business was new to strategic planning and that the team had never had any prior exposure to this type of thinking. However, we decided to jump in the deep end and include key people on the basis that we wanted to develop our team.

"Jimmy is the most senior of the IT consultants and is the logical person to help me with management and delivering on business performance, as well as the product/service area," Tom said. "Livy is keen to introduce personnel systems, so I'd like her to be accountable for that area. With Willy being Dylan IT's Finance and Administration Manager, it is logical that he would oversee the development of our key business systems. And then Charlie as Sales Manager for the business could champion marketing and sales."

"To keep with our metaphor of your journey to the Fourth Moon, Tom, why don't we refer to your top five business goals as Mission Goals?" I suggested.

"I'm fine with that. It makes sense to refer to the reengineering of Dylan IT as a mission with the team. Everyone understands what a mission is, and there is a pioneering aspect to it, which they'll relate to," Tom said.

"You mean your crew," I continued.

"Yes. The crew. Crew members on our mission to the Fourth Moon," Tom said, thinking out loud.

"The crew members could have Crew Goals that Livy will create. Crew Goals would be the crew members' individual top five goals to focus on. Achievement of the Crew Goals would contribute to the achievement of the business's Mission Goals."

"Love it," said Tom. "Let's use these terms to make it more fun and bring the metaphor to life within the business."

We agreed that we wouldn't establish deadlines for the achievement of Mission Goals until the end of the financial year, so that we could implement and bed them down without unrealistic time pressures.

So here are Dylan IT's draft Mission Goals for the year ahead with Internal Champions noted. Tom proudly wrote them down on a small flash card to be kept in his top pocket.

1. **Business Performance**—Implementation of Mission Plan. Deliver Mission Goals. Tom/Jimmy

2. **Products and Services**—Review and develop products/services, pricing, and market. Jimmy

3. **Crew**—Develop, document, and implement individual Crew Goals. Livy

4. **Systems**—Develop, document, and implement business systems and processes. Willy

5. **Marketing and Sales**—Develop and implement a Marketing Plan and sales-based activities to communicate with niche market and hit revenue targets. Charlie

Tom and I agreed to build budgets, targets, and key performance indicators for the business moving forward. We agreed to set up reporting systems with Willy Finance to measure our actual performance.

Tom and I would next review Dylan IT's business model, assess the market, and develop strategies to own that market.

MISSION LOG

Exploring Io: Developing Strategy

- Tom arrives on Io, the First Moon of strategy, and starts his journey to the Fourth Moon.

- Tom learns that his strategy must be documented in a Mission Plan.

- We identify that at the heart of the Mission Plan are the top five goals. These are called Mission Goals.

- Tom sets the Mission Goals for Dylan IT for the year ahead.

- Tom chooses Internal Champions, the specific crew members accountable for achieving a particular Mission Goal.

- Tom commits to defining another set of goals, the top five goals for each individual crew member, and calls these Crew Goals. The achievement of Crew Goals leads to the achievement of Mission Goals.

CHAPTER 6

Selling Tickets: Products, Services, Pricing, and Fulfillment

"I feel as if things are moving too fast," Tom complained. "We're really busy at the moment, and I've got customer issues up to my ears. Can we hold off this First Moon work on strategy for a while?"

"We can't defer any longer, Tom. You're on the First Moon. You committed to this. It's been two weeks since our last meeting. So you and the team have had some time to discuss this while still being able to attend to operational matters."

"You're right, Darren," Tom surrendered, looking like a guilty schoolboy who'd been caught out by the teacher.

Tom was putting up some resistance to rethinking his strategy. Arriving on the First Moon always did this to owners and their management teams. And it made sense. They had their own paradigm of business. Suddenly someone arrives, offering a totally different business paradigm. It can feel uncomfortable—even confrontational—when an outsider recommends that you need to review your strategy and reengineer your business.

There is a massive amount of conditioning and attachment to continuing to do things "the way we always have." It takes courage and self-belief to acknowledge this. This attachment is buried deep within our human psychology. It's like a protective shell that stops us from admitting we're wrong. Conversely, individuals may hold the misplaced belief that it protects them from others seeing they're wrong. The professional ego has a strong hold over the way we project ourselves to the world.

As a result of this conditioning and professional ego, there can be initial conflict on the First Moon. It's amazing how many people around you will be resistant to change, so be prepared for push-back. Beyond you as owner, this resistance can extend internally from management to line staff, and on through to external advisers and even family.

It was going to be tricky to get Tom started with his strategic realignment. The first step was to get him thinking in a new way about his products and services.

"Selling your products and services, Tom, is really just like selling tickets for travel," I proposed. He looked up and gestured for me to continue.

"There are a number of cheap economy-flight tickets to local destinations available for less than a hundred dollars. Then there are the Virgin Galactic personal space-travel tickets that are available for a mere $250,000. They're both tickets to travel; it's just that one ticket is under a hundred bucks, and the other is a quarter of a million bucks," I said.

"So what are they selling, and how do they differ?" I asked him.

"The airline is selling domestic travel to a local destination. Virgin is selling travel into outer space," Tom replied.

"That's right, Tom. But there's more to it," I said. "The discount airline is selling a commodity—in this case local transport, based purely on price. It has only price as a lever, and it has to compete with many competitors in its marketplace.

"On the other hand, Virgin Galactic is selling an experience. It is based not on price, but on a myriad of factors including scarcity, exclusivity, uniqueness, status, and memorability. Virgin Galactic has few, if any, genuine competitors.

"In order to develop your strategy, then, you need to review the tickets you sell: your products and services. How do you charge? What does the customer receive? What does Dylan IT look like to the market? What are the unique features and benefits that your products and services offer over others available? What is the 'it' in Dylan IT?"

Tom expanded on Dylan IT as historically being a service-based business. The vast majority of revenue, he said, was derived from the labor hours charged by the IT team for consulting services. There were some additional small margins on reselling software and hardware. This meant that Tom currently had only one primary revenue stream.

"Let's look at Dylan IT as a service business and then as a product business," I suggested.

"But before we do, though, recall that Jimmy Operations is our Internal Champion on the Mission Goal of reviewing our products, services, and market. Are you comfortable with asking him in with us to discuss this? I think we need to introduce him to this now so that he feels involved from the start. Effective delegation requires good timing. What do you think, Tom?"

Tom agreed. "If we're going to hold him accountable for this area, I think you're right in having his involvement and input right from the get-go."

Jimmy Operations joined us, and we got down to the important task of reviewing the pros and cons of service-based and product-based businesses.

I explained to Jimmy Operations that service-based businesses had distinct advantages, starting with the fact that Dylan IT had been relatively inexpensive to start. As founder, Tom had technical skills, which he developed during earlier employment. As owner-operator, Tom was able to monetize these services immediately through his own labor.

"You didn't have to hire other staff in the start-up phase," I said. "This one-man show allowed you initially to work from home and then later from small business premises. The business costs were minimal at this point. The other benefit was that you were able to attract customers to Dylan IT from your former employee role."

"So they were the positives, what of the negatives?" Jimmy asked, listening intently.

"The negatives of service businesses are numerous. As founder of the business, Tom, you are seen by your customers as the key person. It is difficult to wean them off you and recruit employees to replace you. Business income is based on the hours worked, multiplied by an hourly charge rate.

The flaw in this traditional model is that revenue is effectively capped by the number of available chargeable hours and the market-driven hourly rates that customers are prepared to pay.

"Furthermore, the service business is not as scalable as product businesses—it's not easy to keep adding to employee headcount. As employee headcount grows significantly, so too does the management and infrastructure required to oversee it. To build scale within your service model requires hiring additional labor. This introduces recruitment costs and higher wage costs. There may not be available skilled labor in the market for your services, so recruiting talent may also be challenging. You have to win new business to recover revenue against your wage costs. You have to manage, train, and administrate the hired labor. There is also the added stress and pressure of ensuring your new staff members are productive, and that time charged is fully recoverable from customers. It is hard to escape this 'hours times rate' capped equation."

"That's all fair comment," Tom said, "but can you tell Jimmy and me more about the product business model?"

"Product business models have many advantages," I said. "Revenue is not capped, because the business can be scaled up as customers demand more products. Earning capability is not capped at 'billed hours multiplied by hourly charge rate,' as it is in the service model. After all, there are only so many hours in a day. Subject to product availability and demand, product-based businesses can sell vast volumes of product. There are fewer obstacles to the business. Revenue can be grown aggressively without dramatic increases in wage costs. Geographical boundaries often do not exist in a global economy. The digital age has changed the landscape with online sales channels. The ability to have a range of different products is also an advantage, as this broadens demand and diversifies risk."

"And the negatives?" Jimmy asked.

"The negatives of a product-based business include the fact that the founder must fund the initial cost of manufacturing or purchase of finished product. Unlike in service businesses, products normally require up-front funding. Other unique factors in selling products include warehousing, distribution, product returns, insurance, and the threat of innovation causing product obsolescence. New competitors entering the market can also be a threat."

"I like the idea of diversifying our revenue mix, Darren," Jimmy said. "The constant pressure to capture the billable hours of the IT consultants, invoice the job, and convert it to cash is never-ending. I'm sure Tom would agree that our billing and recovery processes aren't strong. Our productivity across the board isn't great. How can we change our revenue mix to escape this battle?"

"There is no wrong or right in choosing a service- or product-based business model," I said. "The main point to ponder is exploring the option of offering both products and services. In selling products and services, risk can be mitigated and revenue diversified through having a number of offerings for your market.

"I'm suggesting you change the sales mix to build product sales as a percentage of total revenue," I said. "One of your Mission Goals is to conduct a complete review of products and services with Jimmy. I think you need to determine your preferred product/service mix and then target your ideal niche."

Tom had been listening intently, and I could see that he'd never thought about his business model in this way. He'd started the business as a solo IT consultant. As he got more customers, he hired people. It frustrated him that his business revenue was capped by "hours times rate." Tom was personally spending most of his available time doing hands-on consulting with little available time for marketing the business and winning new customers. He knew his team wasn't nearly as productive as they should be, and this annoyed him. Sure, he sold some products, but this was simply reselling software and hardware, and he cringed to think of the modest margins he was charging customers.

For the first time, Tom saw himself as a one-trick pony, selling hours for dollars. He was working just as hard now as when he originally established the business. It all made sense, now, why he was stuck. The capped income model of his IT services business was a jail without bars.

TOM'S CURRENT PRICING MODEL

Tom's IT consultants were on an average hourly wage of $40. The average charge-out rate to customers was $120 per hour. On the face of it, Tom was making $80 per hour on each of his nine IT consultants. But was he really?

Tom, Jimmy, and I did some analysis on the productive labor of his team of IT consultants. To do this, we compared the hours charged to customers against the total hours paid in wages. To Tom's and Jimmy's surprise, they discovered that only 50% of the consulting team's time was charged to customers. So for every two hours of wages paid, the business charged only one hour to the customer. Therefore with only 50% of total labor being productive, the IT consultants had to work two hours at the average wage of $40 per hour to bill the customer one hour at $120. That meant the average cost of labor was actually $80 ($40 per hour multiplied by 2 hours).

The business was in reality only making a gross profit of $40 per hour ($120 charged to customer, less $80 real cost of wages). This $40 gross profit per hour was, of course, before writing off any unrecoverable fees and before any general overhead expenses were deducted for administrative staff wages, rent, computer expenses, motor vehicles, advertising, telephone, or the myriad other costs of running the business.

Tom's jaw dropped. He'd never analyzed this properly. No wonder he wasn't getting ahead. Sure he drew a wage, but he wasn't getting significant profits out of the business, and hadn't yet built any real wealth for himself outside of the business.

"What about pricing and profit for the product-based business?" he asked.

"The pricing and profit relationship for a product business is in comparing the 'average sell price' against the 'average product cost,'" I said. "For manufacturers, average product cost is the cost of raw materials, direct labor, and production. For businesses purchasing products as finished goods, average product cost is the total cost of the product landed into store, including purchase cost, duties, freight, and other direct costs of acquisition. Product businesses apply a margin on the average product cost to set their market price."

"So how can we fix our pricing problems, Darren?" Tom said. "Something has to be done."

"I understand our analysis of prices shows that they have to go up, Tom, but before we address that, I want you to think about where you want your prices to sit within the industry."

"Upper middle to high," Tom said.

"We'll need to look at that when we review your customer base and market. But for the time being, let's stay on this pricing dilemma," I suggested.

ALTERNATIVE PRICING METHODOLOGY

I wanted to let the impact of the products and services discussion settle with Tom and Jimmy Operations, but it was important to keep the strategy discussions moving forward.

"Are you a price-maker or a price-taker?" I asked Tom.

"What do you mean?"

"A price-maker is able to set prices independently, with their customer base willing to pay at this level. A price-taker has their prices determined by market forces, and is dependent on industry norms and customer spending thresholds."

Tom immediately knew the implications of this. He was currently a price-taker. Not only that, but he was caught in a single-offering service business with revenue capped by chargeable hours.

I challenged Tom to consider his customers' psychology in determining the value proposition offered by his team. How did the customers, in their minds, value what Dylan IT delivered? Did Tom educate his customers on what he actually delivered to them? Was there a unique selling proposition that differentiated Tom's business from his competitors, or was he just like the competition?

Jimmy Operations asked how certain service providers could charge at the high end of the market while others discount and price gouge. He felt that some competitors provided the same service yet were able to recover higher fees. I explained that it was a process of educating customers about Dylan IT's value proposition.

"Don't talk about processes, Jimmy, talk about outcomes. You need to add value and deliver outcomes that make you invaluable in the eyes of your customer. Part of this is providing a great service offering and having an engaged and accountable team, but beyond this you need to listen to your customers' pains and dreams, and deliver solutions to them. If you can tune in to customer needs and deliver winning outcomes, while at the same time educating the customer on the value of this proposition, you should be able to charge premium prices in your industry."

I outlined for Jimmy and Tom the revolutionary changes that had been going on in pricing models, specifically the practice of "pricing on value" rather than on hourly rate. The charging of a fixed fee for services has been an innovative approach to tackling the historical problem of the "hourly rates" billing methodology. By charging a service fee that is not based on time spent, a service provider is able to bill revenue based on the value perceived by the customer. If the service provider can demonstrate the value in the services he provides, rather than the time spent on those services, customers will be willing to pay for the service on a basis other than hourly rate. For example, talented graphic designers are likely to charge a fee appropriate to the creative elements they bring to developing a logo, brand, and corporate image. Their price is valued based on the outcome the customer receives rather than time spent. This allows the service provider to introduce efficiencies, economies, and innovation that may allow the service to be either provided in less time or for a higher price—both of which increase profitability. This pricing methodology escapes the paradigm of time-based charges.

"In reviewing your pricing levels, you essentially have three choices," I said. "You can increase price, leave prices unchanged, or decrease your prices. There are many determinants to consider in this decision. Just because you want to increase your prices to boost profits, you need to ask if the market and your customers would be prepared to pay higher prices at this point in time. The general premise is that before you can increase price and charge at the high end of the market, you need to deliver superior services or products. In your case, you need to completely reengineer your business and reeducate your target market before you can charge rates at the top end of the market."

TOM'S PRICING DILEMMA

Once the business had positioned price at the appropriate level, it would be prudent to perform pricing reviews on an annual basis in the future. The future annual debate as to increasing price, keeping prices static, or decreasing prices would have much to do with whether the business had positioned itself as a price-maker or price-taker.

Services

Looking at the average hourly charge-out rate of $120, Tom believed this could be increased by $10 to an average hourly rate of $130 without any resistance from existing customers or the wider target market (he even believed this could be pushed up to $150 over time). Based on approximately 10,000 current charged hours across the business per annum, this $10 per hour increase would yield a $100,000 increase in profit for Dylan IT (10,000 hours at $10 per hour price increase). This $100,000 would be a significant boost to annual profit for such a modest hourly rate increase.

But it wasn't all about price. The 50% productivity of the consulting team was appalling. Most service businesses operated at productivity rates significantly higher than that. Recovering just one hour of income out of every two hours of paid labor just wasn't going to cut it. Imagine the impact if the company could get chargeable hours up from 50% to 75%, move to higher-end pricing over time, and create a powerful marketing message that won Dylan IT an abundance of new customers. The opportunities were endless, and the light bulb had certainly flicked on in Tom's brain.

I encouraged Tom and Jimmy to try and get an annual price increase at least equal to inflation and wage growth. In doing so, they would keep profit levels protected in "present day dollars" so profit wouldn't be eroded through wage growth and inflation. There is a science to educating customers on price increases and training them to expect annual increases. I suggested that Dylan IT communicate price increases to customers in advance. It can be done verbally or in writing, but I prefer writing. An email or letter sent out three months in advance of the price increase softens the blow and demonstrates professionalism and respect. The timing of annual price increases is best done at the start of the financial year or on the anniversary of an annual or periodic contract term.

Products

I asked Tom about the products sold through the business. These were currently the mainstream software and hardware products typically used by the small- to medium-business sector. However, Tom also provided some customized databases and customer relationship management modules (CRMs). I couldn't believe it when Tom explained he merely added a small handling fee of 5% to these items on customers' bills.

The worst part was that Tom scoped and sourced the software and the hardware requirements using his IT expertise. He handled the supply logistics—including storage, delivery, and installation. It pained me that Tom charged just 5% for all of this.

Tom felt there wouldn't be oversensitivity from customers if he increased the price of products, as they made up the smaller portion of a project cost. The service side of the transaction for consulting time was the significant percentage of total cost. On that basis, Tom was prepared to immediately increase his product margin, from the existing 5% to 10%. This would effectively double the profit margin on future product sales overnight.

Fulfillment

For Dylan IT, fulfillment is the business's ability to deliver its service effectively and efficiently to its market on time, at cost, and with expected quality. As demand grows, so does the business's need for human talent. The ability to recruit talented labor with the skills and attitude required to deliver specialized services is limited. If there is a shortage of IT consultants in the industry and the business is growing dramatically, the talent pool may not deliver the number of new employees required to service market demand. The ceiling for charge-out rates accepted within the industry is also a limiting factor.

Productivity was also a significant challenge for Dylan IT. Recall that Tom's business currently has a miserly productivity rate of 50% chargeable hours. How would he motivate a growing team to care about charging for all of their time? How would he ensure all members of his service team were performing the right activities? Is the time spent by each employee recoverable? If mistakes are made, they're generally discovered later, with that lost time being unrecoverable. Tom must get individuals to be accountable for their time and record it accurately.

Quality assurance is a major challenge in fulfillment for a service business. Customers are outcome focused, so they look only at what they get, not at how they get it. They're not interested in understanding how Tom manages quality from his employees. They care about the lousy job Dylan IT just did for them. And it's Tom's problem, as owner, to fix it.

Managing lead-times becomes tricky as a service business grows. Ever tried to see an accountant at short notice? They're often booked out weeks in advance. What if an important new client opportunity or existing client issue comes up that needs immediate attention? The client's expectation on lead-time is now, whereas the service business's lead-time is subject to availability. This time difference can be described as the "expectation gap."

The invisibility of service fulfillment can also cause these expectation gaps. A lack of understanding by customers of the services performed, charge-out rates, and time delays between service delivery and rendering of an invoice can all cause issues in recoverability.

For product businesses, assessing fulfillment holds different challenges and opportunities. The major fulfillment dilemma is how to get the product to the customer in the most timely and cost-effective manner. Physical products need to be manufactured or shipped into stores. Both of these sourcing processes involve lead-times. Again, the customer doesn't think about lead-times. Tom would like them to, but they don't! The customer has his own expectations (right or wrong) about how quickly the product will arrive in his hands. From a product fulfillment perspective, the Dylan IT team must manage these expectations and close the expectation gap.

Tom had seemed a little overwhelmed by my comments on selecting the right business model, reviewing his services and products, and his pricing and fulfillment. However, he was upbeat about the pricing changes and the impact they would have on profit. The introduction of a wider range of products and services to the business service offering was also a key opportunity. We agreed to tackle improving fulfillment with better project management and increased productivity through higher chargeable hours, which were just some of the take-aways Tom had discovered in our session together.

"We'd like you to be responsible for reviewing and reengineering products, services, pricing, and fulfillment," Tom proposed to Jimmy Operations.

"It's a big project, but I'm going to need your help on this, Jimmy. As you said, something's gotta change. We can't keep going on this hamster wheel. We've got to break free. Are you up for the challenge?"

"I'll need some direction," Jimmy said. "And I'll certainly need more access to you, Tom. You know how hard it is to catch up together."

"I know. I know," Tom replied. "I've become acutely aware of my short-comings recently. I assure you that things are going to change around this place, and it starts with me. I'll make the time, and feel free to hassle me if I resist."

"Okay, I will," Jimmy confirmed. "When do we start?"

"You can certainly start thinking about it now, Jimmy," I said. "Perhaps start taking some notes, mapping out ideas, and reviewing our competitors' business models. However, Tom and I still have a bit of work to do in reviewing our customer base, niche market, the Dylan IT team, and our overall business functionality. Once we've done that, we want to meet with you, Livy, Charlie, and Willy to formally launch the Dylan IT strategy. That sound all right with you?"

"Makes sense, I guess. Given where we are coming from, I don't think we should go off half-cocked on these changes. It has to be done properly," Jimmy said.

"Good for you, Jimmy," Tom stated. "I might catch up with you later. Darren and I need to wrap things up now."

As Jimmy Operations walked out of the boardroom more purposefully than he had entered, I turned to Tom.

"What did you think?" I prompted.

"Jimmy spoke honestly. We are stuck. He's right. It's a huge job, but I think he's up to it," Tom said.

"I do too, Tom. Jimmy will be fine. But stick to your promise and make the time to meet with him regularly when we've landed on the Second Moon, Europa—implementation."

While on Io, a comprehensive review of the products and services that Dylan IT offered the market, with the desired sales mix determined, was part of the important strategic infrastructure work. Io's geological activity had certainly challenged Tom, and today's discussions had been quite over-whelming at times.

The next part of the infrastructure to be established was the defining of Dylan IT's ideal niche. In conjunction with the selection of products and services to be offered to the market, Tom had to decide which market to serve.

The good news was that Tom had let go of his initial defensiveness. The rational side of his professional ego had taken over and realized that developing strategy on the First Moon was the first important step toward serious change. He was invested. Tom's resistance, negativity, and cynicism had melted away like butter on a hot pan. Now he had the mental capacity to let in new ideas, reengineer his strategy, and break away from being stuck.

Before leaving, I empathized with Tom that Galileo's attitudes of patience and open-mindedness would be constantly tested while on the First Moon.

Tom would indeed need Galileo by his side on this stage of his journey.

MISSION LOG

Selling Tickets: Products, Services, Pricing, and Fulfillment

- Tom realizes Dylan IT is a service-based business that desperately needs to change its sales mix.

- Tom and Jimmy Operations review Dylan IT pricing and discover that current pricing, poor productivity, and weak internal systems have dramatically eroded profit.

- Tom is disappointed to learn that Dylan IT is a price-taker rather than a price-maker, with the business selling hours for dollars rather than pricing on value.

- Tom reviews his service model, deciding to increase hourly charge-out rates and significantly increase the productivity of the crew.

- Tom reviews current product pricing and increases the margin charged to customers.

- Tom asks Jimmy Operations if he will be responsible for reviewing and reengineering products, services, pricing, and fulfillment (Mission Goal #2). Jimmy accepts.

CHAPTER 7

Passengers: Business Class, Economy, and Freight

"We haven't talked in detail about your customers, Tom."

"If it wasn't for them," Tom quipped with a cheeky smile, "running this business would be a whole lot easier."

Tom expanded on his customers, reflecting on "the good, the bad, and the just plain ugly."

He said, "The good customers appreciate the time, effort, and skills our team delivers. They display integrity, are easygoing and respectful, and pay us on time. The bad customers are high maintenance. They drop by without notice and expect us to drop everything. They are rude and impatient with staff and don't pay on time. The ugly are simply impossible to please. They tell me nothing and pay me nothing. It's like doing a thousand-piece jigsaw puzzle without showing me the picture on the box." Tom shook his head in frustration.

CUSTOMER STOCKTAKE

"Let's do a stocktake of your customers, Tom," I suggested, "and rank them from A to E."

We grouped Tom's "good" customers into A's and B's, the "bad" customers into C's and D's. Of course, the "ugly" customers were E's.

I suggested we imagine the customers as passengers on our journey. The A and B customers would travel in Business Class and get the full personalized treatment. The C and D customers would travel in Economy, receiving good solid service without the frills. The E customers would have to be stowaways in Freight or hit the road and hitch.

I explained the goal of winning more Business Class customers, moving Economy customers into Business Class, and simply not working for Freight customers. If C and D customers couldn't pay the price of an Economy ticket, they would become Freight customers and not be serviced.

Tom smiled. He liked the idea of a regular customer stocktake. I thought I saw a glazed look of perverse delight creep over his face as he mentally listed the E customers he'd soon pack in Freight. He even rubbed his chin in deliberation!

We then analyzed the frequency with which customers utilized Dylan IT services. It was pleasing to see that Business Class customers used Dylan IT's services most frequently. We then reviewed the "annual spend" by customers. Again, we discovered that the top annual spenders were also Business Class customers.

I went on to explain that the lifetime value of a customer is simply the number of years a customer is retained multiplied by the customer's average annual spend. For example, if a customer spends $20,000 each year with you and you retain that customer for seven years, then the lifetime value of that customer is $140,000 ($20,000 multiplied by 7 years). The idea is to win more A and B customers, increase their average job value and annual spend, and retain them for many years.

With this strategy alone, Tom was able to immediately look at his customer base in a whole new way. He committed to immediately sacking customers that were Freight. If the Economy customers couldn't be moved to Business Class over time, he would assess whether he would service them. If a customer didn't respect Tom and his team, work constructively, and pay on time, they simply wouldn't be a customer of Dylan IT.

Tom gasped. "How good would that feel?"

Tom also reflected on the impact of having fewer customers; he concluded that that would make things easier to manage and service. His back-office administration would also be reduced. More Business Class customers would mean improved workflow, profitability, and cash flow. From a team perspective, productivity would increase with improved scope of work and job satisfaction. Project management would also be easier.

"If I do a proper customer stocktake, the Freight customers can join that competitor I told you about—Peter Perfect. Word on the street is that Peter has been approaching my customers and going pretty hard for their business," Tom confided.

Tom went on to explain that his nemesis, Peter Perfect, was offering deep discounts and a support package that Tom felt wouldn't be honored. Initially, Tom had resisted acknowledging this with customers as he didn't like conflict and wanted to avoid being seen overtly criticizing Peter.

Now, however, Tom felt like he had a strategic and rational way to combat Peter Perfect. He could focus on his own best customers, and let Peter have the rest. Tom was also about to discover that serving a niche market would further combat Peter Perfect.

NICHE

"Now that we know the type of customers we want, let's look at your niche," I suggested to Tom.

"My niche?" Tom asked. "Won't I lose customers if I change my niche? Isn't it too late to overhaul my customer base?"

"The good news is, Tom, that it's never too late. Most business owners keep running on autopilot. They never analyze themselves, their businesses, or their performance. They just buy a job and drift along, never really achieving success."

I explained to Tom the need to bed down strategy on the First Moon. Nailing your niche was part of creating a strategy. No one gets to the Fourth Moon without a strong niche. Make no mistake, the fact that so few owners reach the Fourth Moon just highlights how many businesses haven't thought through their niche, let alone targeted it.

A market niche is the target group of customers that you strategically aim to serve. Your aim is to offer products and services that satisfy the specific target market's needs. Tom's assessment of his current market niche was both brutal and honest. He seemed to service almost any small to medium business requiring IT services. He realized that his current target market was much, much too broadly defined.

"What if I told you the narrower your niche, the better?" I proposed to Tom.

"That seems mad," Tom responded. "Why would I limit my opportunities to win new customers by appealing to fewer people?"

"Ah," I said. "That's the really cool bit. It doesn't."

I let Tom momentarily digest this conundrum.

"At first it seems counterintuitive," I said, pausing.

I continued. "How could narrowing your target market create more customers? A natural response to this is fear. Most people's immediate response is to think that by targeting a narrower niche, there are fewer prospects. Fewer prospects means fewer customers. Fewer customers means less income. And then you go broke. That's right isn't it?

"The good news is it's not the case," I said. "The narrower the niche, the better. By having a narrower niche, you are able to communicate in a much more targeted way. You can develop consistent niche messages that create awareness about your business. Over time, prospects within your niche learn about your expertise and develop an awareness of your products and services. While the total pool of these prospects may be smaller in number, the number of those prospects that will buy from you is much greater. Not only that, businesses with focused niches are generally able to command higher prices.

"That is why less is more, Tom."

"Can you give me some examples?" Tom asked, clearly not convinced just yet.

"Sure," I said. I outlined some examples for Tom. "Sue was a former executive who had been a successful corporate high-flyer before having a child. After her baby was born, Sue struggled to return to the corporate workforce. She decided she wanted to start her own business as an executive coach. Rather than compete against all the other executive coaches targeting the broad corporate market, Sue decided to target a narrow niche. The niche she chose was senior female executives from the largest 100 corporations wishing to return to the workforce after maternity leave. This immediately differentiated her from virtually all the competition. She understood her niche. Let's face it, her niche was filled with women in situations like her own. Sue could communicate and empathize with her target market as a true expert. Whether speaking or writing, Sue was able to relate to the struggle of a high-flying corporate mom attempting to return to the workforce while maintaining a good family life."

"So how did Sue succeed?" Tom asked leaning forward.

"She was a huge success. She needed only a small number of senior executive women as customers at any one time, women from the largest 100 corporations. These strong, independent women valued the services of a mentor, coach, and confidante. After all, Sue was one of them. They were happy to pay a premium for such a specialized service. Not only that, they spread the word among their professional network and peers. Within eighteen months, Sue had a waiting list. Suddenly, becoming a customer was upon invitation. Sue had an army of walking billboards promoting her business. Even better, Sue understood the corporate employers. She acknowledged these corporations' reservations, fears, and expectations of returning female executives. So Sue worked with them and their teams. Sue was engaged as a guest speaker, invited to participate in focus groups, and asked to work directly with female executives by the corporate employers. Within three years, Sue was recognized as the only go-to expert in her niche market."

"Wow," said Tom.

"Let me give you a couple of other examples. Michael was an electrical contractor. Rather than be a general electrician, Michael specialized in the food industry. In doing so, he became the niche provider of electrical equipment and services for the food industry. This narrow niche offered high-value projects at better margins.

"Then there was Paul the lawyer. Paul was an expert in intellectual property law, and worked with many businesses in the creative world of graphic art, advertising, and media. Paul's law firm specialized in protecting the intellectual property of 'creatives' within this niche. Paul is seen as an expert in his niche and is sought after as a speaker, commentator, and adviser."

Tom suddenly realized the power of having a narrower niche. "It seems so much easier to target your market," Tom said. "Prospects would be more willing to engage an expert, and to pay more for a specialist."

He went on, "I can see how this works. But how do I narrow my niche?"

Niche Talents

It suddenly dawned on me that while we had done a broad stocktake of Tom's customers, we hadn't performed a thorough analysis of Tom's background and niche talents.

"Understanding your most suitable niche, Tom, is often about understanding yourself. In the niche examples I gave you, all those business owners had one thing in common. Choosing your niche typically involves finding something you love doing, something you're good at, and something you innately understand. The first two points are a given. However, the third point about understanding your niche comes from specific exposure or industry experience. Often people are sitting on their ideal niche without even realizing it."

I could see Tom was close to a breakthrough. I wanted to explore Tom's personal journey more and see how this might tie in to helping him develop his niche.

"Tom, we've talked mostly about your business. But what about you personally? As we've discussed, the best niche is something authentic to you."

Tom elaborated on his personal background. His father had run a manufacturing business. When computers came in, Tom started playing with basic databases and early business applications.

"Dad always had problems with tracking his inventory accurately," Tom said. "Trying to keep it up to date manually was a tedious task. He also wanted better ways to measure his cost of production through analyzing raw materials and labor. I developed some early programs that allowed Dad to know his cost of raw materials and hourly labor rates. I suppose this early exposure led me to studying information technology at university. After uni, I got a job in IT, working in the manufacturing and distribution sector. My early time working with Dad helped me understand importing, exporting, manufacturing, and distribution. As an employee, I tinkered in developing

IT solutions tailored to the manufacturing and distribution sector. Several of these programs are still used by customers today."

I was captivated by Tom's story.

"So how did you transition from employee to business owner?" I asked Tom.

"I got frustrated with not being in control of my own destiny, I suppose. I felt an increasing desire to be my own boss and to service customers the way I wanted to."

"So what happened?" I asked. "How did you get started?"

"I backed myself, I guess. I saved a bit, I had a few private customers that I worked with outside of work hours, and I thought a few customers might join me if I started out on my own. As it turned out, people supported me, and the business was born."

"Were most of those customers from the manufacturing and distribution sector?" I probed.

"Yes," Tom said, "most of them were. They appreciated my knowledge of the industry and were keen to hire someone who understood what they did."

"Are any of those customers still with you?"

"Oh definitely," Tom stated emphatically. "They're nearly all still with me."

"Are these customers A's and B's under our classification?" I asked.

"Those guys are definitely A's and B's, no problem. They're still a pleasure to deal with, and so loyal. They've become friends over the years."

"So what percentage of your customer base is from the manufacturing and distribution sector?"

"About a third," Tom stated. "Customers in that sector get the platinum service. They get a lot of free software, databases, and operational configurations from us."

"Free?" I asked. "Don't you charge extra for that?"

"No. I just charge our time and provide all of that as part of the service."

I was floored. Tom was clearly an expert in IT services for the manufacturing and distribution sector. He had developed intellectual property over ten to fifteen years that was being used widely, and yet he wasn't being paid for it.

"So, I think we have discovered your niche, Tom," I said smiling broadly.

Tom raised his eyebrows. "We have?"

"What if you were able to service the manufacturing and distribution sector exclusively? Imagine charging industry specialist rates for your expertise. Further, what if you branded the software and databases you developed, and charged your customers for this? In addition, you could provide annual support and updates for an additional fee. Only customers in the manufacturing and distribution sector could work with you. You could promote your services through their industry associations and professional networks. How would your business look then?"

Tom was speechless. He'd been sitting on his ideal niche without even knowing it. Worse still, he hadn't charged higher fees as an expert, or charged customers for his proprietary software and databases. I could see Tom was a little melancholy as this realization set in. He wore his heart on his sleeve, and it was bleeding a bit.

"Are you prepared to transition your business into the niche of being a specialist IT provider exclusive to the manufacturing and distribution sector?" I asked Tom.

Tom perked up. "Yeah, I think I can do it, Darren. It will take some changes, and I don't want to sack customers overnight or polarize my staff. But it can be done. And as for Peter Perfect, he can't compete strongly against me in this niche."

Just the immediacy of Tom's solemn and measured acknowledgment was enough to satisfy me for the day. It had been a major breakthrough for him and for both of us in our work together.

"One last question before you go," Tom said. "How do I own my niche?"

"Good question, Tom. Now that we've defined your niche, we'll develop your niche message and a battery of methods for communicating this with the manufacturing and distribution sector. This can be addressed when we focus on marketing and sales later, while we're still on the First Moon. But for the moment, take a break and enjoy the satisfaction of knowing your niche. Most business owners don't!"

MISSION LOG

Passengers: Business Class, Economy, and Freight

- Tom conducts a customer stocktake, grouping customers into categories of Good (A, B), Bad (C, D), and Ugly (E).

- The A and B customers are Business Class, the C and D customers are Economy, and the E customers are Freight.

- Tom agrees to focus on attracting more Business Class passengers, moving Economy passengers into Business Class, and sacking Freight passengers.

- Tom understands the narrower his niche, the better.

- Tom realizes his niche talents lie in the selling of software, hardware, and specialized services to the manufacturing and distribution sector.

- Tom agrees to transition the business into this niche.

CHAPTER 8

Radio Frequency: Tuning In to Your Niche

"So what's left to do on the First Moon, Darren?" Tom asked as I entered his boardroom for our next meeting.

"Remember that we discovered your niche last time we met up together?" I said.

"How could I forget!" Tom enthused. "I haven't been able to stop thinking about it."

"You discovered that your true niche is in providing IT products and services to the manufacturing and distribution sector. Now that you know that, we need to create a niche message. What are the issues, obstacles, and opportunities that occupy the lives of your niche market participants? If your niche message addresses these things, it will resonate with customers and prospects in your niche."

Tom paused for a moment and then said, "My customers are importers, manufacturers, and distributors. It's all about moving product. They're interested in production, inventory, supply chain, and logistics. There is product range, seasonality, and trend. Costing and pricing are critical. Databases capturing product specifications, cost/price inputs, and customer relation-ship management (CRM) data are integral to their operation."

"That's exactly what I'm talking about," I stated emphatically to Tom. "Let's get started."

I spoke to Tom at length about the concept of "helping, not selling." Our style should be authentic communication with integrity. Underlying our communication style needs to be content that is rich in value and helps our niche customers operate their businesses. If communication style and con-tent are consistent throughout the business, it doesn't matter whether we're interacting with customers, prospects, employees, suppliers, or shareholders.

"If our style is helping, not selling, how do we sell to them?" Tom asked.

"Through our niche message and content," I responded. "We know our niche customers are manufacturers and distributors. Our style will be to help them rather than to sell or pitch them. So the strategy is to communicate a consistent message that helps our niche solve their problems and eliminate their headaches. If you do this consistently, Tom, manufacturers and distrib-utors will see you as an expert in your field. Strangers will become prospects. Prospects will become customers."

We workshopped how we could help manufacturers and distributors through creating rich and practical content. This would become our market-ing collateral. Tom highlighted some generic problems faced by manufactur-ers and distributors.

But first, I wanted to clarify hard-dollar marketing and soft-dollar mar-keting with Tom.

"We now live in the digital age, Tom. Hard-dollar marketing is the spend-ing of real, hard dollars on advertising. While this medium is still alive, it is a shrinking beast. Pre-Internet, it was the only game in town. Television, newspapers, magazines, and business directory advertising swallowed up large budgets. There was little competition. Create a message, and broadcast it to lots of people. This is hard-dollar marketing at work with serious money being spent. It either works or doesn't, and the stakes are high—cash burn."

I went on. "Now, in the Internet age, we live in more enlightened times. There's been a shift from blasting advertising messages at people to provid-ing rich content. Rich content is content that is considered valuable by your target audience. It may interest, educate, or even entertain a prospect. The days of the traditional advertising giant are numbered. Who keeps a printed business directory these days? Who watches ads on TV in the digital age of fighting for eyeball minutes?

"Soft-dollar marketing is an approach that spends little or no money in creating valuable content to market your business," I said. "Rather than the hit-or-miss gamble of hard-dollar marketing, it allows you to test your content and measure the results. Examples include blogs, articles, white papers, e-books, forum posts, social networking (Facebook, Twitter, LinkedIn, etc.), speaking, and traditional printed books. In the digital age, much of this is free and merely requires allocating some time to the creation of valuable content."

I suggested to Tom that we focus on soft-dollar marketing strategies with some allocation of funds for hard-dollar marketing spends. I also requested that we develop a Marketing Plan to outline the actions, frequency, accountability, and implementation of this.

"I think we should get Charlie to workshop this with us, Tom. I know from my initial meetings with him that he wants to have input, and he's clearly keen to help the business. Having his involvement in developing a Marketing Plan would help us get his buy-in on being accountable for delivering it as well. You can't do everything yourself if you want to reach the Fourth Moon. What do you think?"

"Makes sense," Tom said. "I'll go and get him now. I saw he was in this morning."

After Charlie Sales joined us, Tom and I briefed him on the idea of focusing our attention on our niche market—manufacturers and distributors.

Since we had briefed Charlie on the customer stocktake, he was already aware of the need to service A and B customers, transition C and D customers to A and B status, and sack E customers.

He also now understood the power and benefits of the A and B customers exclusively being manufacturers and distributors.

Understandably, Charlie held some fears and anxieties around not servicing existing customers, given he was the retail interface. However, after Tom and I explained that they would be transitioned out of the business over the next twelve months, his fears settled.

We then moved on to discussing the need for the business to develop more products to complement our struggling service model—consulting. Charlie was acutely aware of Dylan IT's current poor service record on billing and recovering consulting hours. He was regularly perplexed by the consultants' apparent disconnect in understanding that their salaries were paid for by billed and recovered consulting time charged to customers. On the other side, Charlie had to face the wrath of exasperated customers venting their displeasure at Dylan IT invoices that would arrive late and without explanation.

"So let me get this straight," Charlie clarified. "Over the next year, Dylan IT is committed to serving manufacturers and distributors exclusively?"

"Yes," Tom confirmed.

"And within that niche, we intend to work with customers that we rate A and B, and perhaps some C and D customers we think we can convert to A and B status?"

Tom nodded. "That's right."

"Within our target niche," Tom continued, "we want to develop more products to complement our existing services. These products will consist of specialized proprietary software for manufacturers and distributors. We will have fixed-price service agreements to complement our software products, which will include training and support."

"What about our current problem with consulting time and recovering billed hours?" Charlie interrupted.

"We get Jimmy, Livy, and Willy to work on a revamped consulting model. They will drive the consultants to record time more accurately, communicate with customers to manage their expectations around cost, and invoice weekly. The entire lead-time of consultant hours to cash at bank will be measured and monitored. Our culture and internal systems have to change, Charlie," Tom said emphatically.

Tom and I could see Charlie liked what he heard.

"So, what else?" Charlie asked.

"We have to put together a Marketing Plan," I insisted. "We need to create a comprehensive suite of information that helps our target market. It must first attract their attention. The content must relate directly to their fears, dreams, and niche needs. We must communicate in a style that is helping, not selling. And finally, it must position Dylan IT in their minds as a specialist IT provider to the manufacturing and distribution sector."

"That sounds like a lot of work, Darren," Tom resisted. "What do we have to do?"

"I'll help create it with you, Tom," Charlie offered with assurance.

"We will need both of you to help. Jimmy and Livy can offer some technical input. And of course, I'll be here to guide and assist you too," I said.

I explained to Tom and Charlie the principle of recycling content.

"Much of the content we will create can be refashioned and recycled for different mediums. Recycling content allows us to use our niche content in different forums of our communication."

"Can you give us an example, Darren?" Charlie asked.

"Okay. Do you guys like movies?" I asked.

Tom and Charlie nodded in unison.

"Well, let's look at how content is recycled around a movie. A movie is the core product that is initially broadcast at a cinema. The production team takes the images and the sounds of the movie and recycles them. They will use this same content to create a dedicated website, a trailer, posters, TV ads, blogs, brochures, YouTube releases, and a whole lot more. After the movie is released, they recycle the whole movie for release on DVD, online, cable, and free-to-air television."

"I'd never thought of it like that before," Charlie said. "So let's workshop this for Dylan IT."

Tom, Charlie, and I set about reviewing the content we needed to create for Dylan IT, with a focus on recycling. Through recycling content, we could cut down on the amount of work required.

These were the initial content distribution channels we developed for our Marketing Plan:

Blog

I wasn't sure if I could get Tom's buy-in to writing a regular blog post. But when he realized he could provide specific tips, commentary, and resources that would interest manufacturers and distributors, he was in.

Tom suggested that Charlie, Jimmy, and Livy could contribute to the blog also. External guest blog contributors might also feature from the manufacturing and distribution sector.

Website

The Dylan IT website desperately needed an overhaul. It didn't communicate a niche message or deliver rich content. It was merely a static brochure site. In committing to a blog, Dylan IT would have continuous dynamic content on the website, providing a reason for previous visitors and new visitors to connect and engage.

"We could set up a registration sign-up box on the website where visitors simply enter their first name and email address. On signing up, they'd receive Tom's blog, sector news, updates, and invitations to educational content. With only ten seconds or less before someone clicks off of a website, it is critical to have this 'call to action' promptly displayed," I suggested.

Brochure

"The website content could be recycled to create a Dylan IT brochure," Charlie added.

"Yes," I encouraged. "The look and feel of the brochure would be consistent with the Dylan IT website."

Many businesses don't have a brochure, and owners often claim they don't need one. However, I recommended the creation of a simple yet professional brochure in hard copy and soft copy. If meeting a prospect in person, Tom and Charlie could leave some physical evidence of their time together. The soft copy would be helpful for attaching to email correspondence. It would also be downloadable from the Dylan IT website.

Articles

"We could also turn our blog posts into articles," Tom suggested. "That would be easy."

I suggested Tom set up a "free resources" or "free stuff" page on his website. If Tom wrote a handful of articles beneficial to manufacturers and distributors, this would provide rich content for visitors to the site. Google and other search engines love rich content, and the inclusion of this on Dylan IT's website would assist in optimizing his organic search ranking.

These articles could also be sent to prospects and the media, and become listed on article websites. Tom could also cross-reference his articles with the "frequently asked questions" (FAQ) page of his website. In addition, he could forward these articles to manufacturing and distribution sector trade publications.

Video

"Don't forget the number one TV station," I teased.

"What station is that?" Charlie asked.

I smiled. "YouTube, of course. Let's set up a Dylan IT YouTube channel. You can create short videos that answer 'how to' questions, offer training on your software, provide tips for manufacturers and distributors, and include other helpful content.

"These videos can be recycled too," I went on. "They can appear on your website, and be easily linked within email and social networking broadcasts."

Social Networking

"I've been thinking about how we can better utilize social networking within the business, Darren. Any ideas here?" Charlie asked.

I discussed social networking with Charlie and Tom, again revisiting the concept of recycling content. In broadcasting on Facebook, Twitter, and LinkedIn, the business could use blog content, article extracts, video, or other niche-centric content to fuel these fires. From these broadcasts, newly engaged niche participants could post on these platforms themselves, creating even richer content organically.

Hard-Dollar Marketing

"So these are what you refer to as soft-dollar marketing activities," Tom said. "What of the hard-dollar marketing options?"

We discussed several traditional hard-dollar marketing areas. Tom and Charlie agreed they might consider approaching industry associations and publications. While they would consider paid advertising, initially they would explore opportunities to contribute content instead. After all, these associations and publications were communicating with the same niche target market—manufacturers and distributors.

Tom suggested we also set up a Google AdWords account and trial a campaign using different keywords. Google AdWords are the paid advertisements that appear when you enter a search term in Google. Depending on the search keywords you sign up for, you pay a certain amount of money each time someone clicks on your advertisement. This is also referred to as "pay-per-click." Tom set a budget for his total spend per month for a six-month period. We agreed to trial a number of keywords targeting manufacturers and distributors, and then to monitor the results through Google's analytical reporting.

Sales-based Activity

"I think you should consider allocating much of your precious hard-dollar spend on your manufacturing and distribution customers and prospects," I suggested.

"The creation of a niche target market, niche message, communication style (helping, not selling), and Marketing Plan should streamline effortlessly into the sales function. We need to work with Charlie to develop a battery of multiple sales activities. We will have rich niche content created through the Marketing Plan, but it's only beneficial if we use this stuff."

Tom and I agreed to split the sales function into prospects (new business) and customers (existing). Prospects would be identified through marketing communication and capturing of email addresses and contact details. If a prospect makes an inquiry or requests more information, Charlie will contact them and offer to have a one-hour free consultation without obligation. This will eliminate the need to cold call or make unsolicited contact with prospects. For existing customers, Tom developed a calendar for Charlie to follow in reaching out to customers on a systematic basis. This would depend on their A, B, or C classification. Tom would include himself in these customer catch-ups on a rotational basis. These customer catch-ups would include site visits, hospitality, training, and events.

Tom and I agreed to set up targets and key performance indicators around the sales-based activities of Charlie on our visits to the Second Moon and Third Moon.

"So how do you feel, Tom?" I asked cautiously.

"Excited, but still a bit scared and overwhelmed," he said, leaning back in his chair.

"What about you, Charlie?"

"I'm pumped," Charlie said excitedly. "I can't wait to get started on this. I can really see this making a difference. We'll have to meet regularly on this, Tom. I want to carry this momentum forward.

"Are you happy if I get started on this now?" Charlie asked.

"Go for your life, Charlie," Tom encouraged. "Come back and see me tomorrow to make a few meeting times for us to catch up on this over the week ahead."

"Will do, Boss," Charlie said as he strode out of the boardroom.

"I think we have a motivated Sales Manager onboard now in Charlie Sales," I said.

"I think we have, Darren. I pity the poor manufacturing and distribution businesses out there that haven't met Charlie yet. They don't know what's going to hit them!"

MISSION LOG

Radio Frequency: Tuning In to Your Niche

- Tom and Charlie review the new niche market Dylan IT will service: manufacturers and distributors.

- Tom and Charlie workshop the development of a Marketing Plan aimed at communicating with their target niche.

- Tom and Charlie learn the difference between soft-dollar and hard-dollar marketing.

- Dylan IT will focus on soft-dollar marketing activities through creating information that helps their niche.

- Dylan IT will recycle their content by communicating it through a range of mediums.

- Charlie agrees to develop a Marketing Plan that includes a blog, website revamp, brochure, articles, video content, and social networking.

CHAPTER 9

Crew: Mission Management

Tom was eager to get our next meeting started. "Now that we've gotten all this strategy stuff out of the way, let's blast off for the Second Moon."

"There's no point rushing to get off the First Moon," I told Tom. "On the First Moon, we need to get our strategy right. Who wants to take a substandard strategy and waste time implementing it on the Second Moon and maintaining it on the Third Moon? Not to mention the fact that there are no leverage opportunities on the Fourth Moon with a poor strategy."

"I get it, Darren, don't worry. I'm hanging in there. But can I ask what is ahead of us while we are still on the First Moon?"

I explained to Tom the importance of structuring our team and developing an approach to managing that team. Beyond this, we still needed to workshop our communication, marketing, and sales function.

Returning the conversation back to the team, I directed our attention to the important foundation blocks of the Organizational Chart.

"Recapping, we defined the Mission Goals upon landing on the First Moon. We'll revisit those shortly when we develop and document the Crew Goals for each team member. We then reengineered your products and services with Jimmy Operations, asking the question of what is the 'it' we want to sell. We then reviewed our customers and decided on our niche of who we want to sell 'it' to. Then most recently, with the help of Charlie Sales, we determined how to sell 'it.'

"So to come back to your question of what's left to do on the First Moon, Tom, there are two areas of our strategy left to rework while we're still on Io."

I continued, "Remember, from now on we're referring to your employees as crew. We need to review our organizational structure, to devise and document Crew Goals that support your Mission Goals. We'll also implement Crew Reviews, which are one-on-one sessions with crew members, in order to appraise and reward their performance.

"Next time we meet up, we'll focus on Mission Management, which will ensure that operational functionality not only exists, but is optimized within Dylan IT."

STRUCTURING THE CREW

Returning the discussion back to the crew, I discussed the crucial role the Organizational Chart plays in business success.

Every organization needs to maintain an Organizational Chart. An Organizational Chart is a graphical diagram depicting the titles, names, and relationships of each positional function within the business. It's surprising most businesses don't have their Organizational Charts documented and kept up to date.

We reviewed Dylan IT's current Organizational Chart, which looked like this:

Organizational Chart for Dylan IT

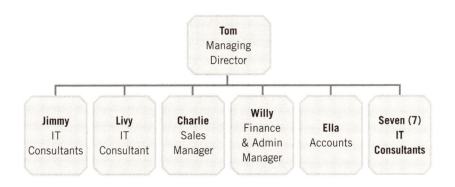

"Let's play with this a bit," I suggested to Tom.

"To recap earlier discussions, you agreed to trial Jimmy as Operations Manager for the business. He can be your 2IC or second-in-charge. So that's Jimmy Operations. Livy is Senior Consultant—effectively your 3IC. She can directly report to Jimmy, with all the IT consultants reporting to her operationally. That would mean Jimmy Operations has Livy Consulting reporting to him. Ella in accounts will report directly to Willy Finance as Finance and Administration Manager. Charlie Sales of course still continues to report directly to you. That's the new management team, Tom.

"This structure will develop the management skills of Jimmy, Livy, and Willy. But the biggest payoff will be for you, Tom. Without twelve direct reports, you can build stronger relationships with customers, win new business, reallocate time to activities of choice, and work fewer hours. You could mentor both Jimmy Operations and Livy Consulting in their operational roles. You could develop a winning sales and marketing strategy with Charlie Sales. And you could focus on the financial and admin side of the business with Willy Finance. Are you comfortable with this scenario?" I asked Tom.

Tom paused and took in a big breath.

"I'm feeling a bit outside my comfort zone, and I can be a bit of a control freak. But yes, I am prepared to give it a go. A proper go," Tom said cautiously.

"That's fair enough, Tom. I can understand letting go is a big step for you right now. But I can assure you that holding on to the status quo isn't the answer."

Tom and I redrafted the Organizational Chart for Dylan IT, now titling it as the Crew Chart, to reflect this. This is what it now looked like:

Crew Chart for Dylan IT

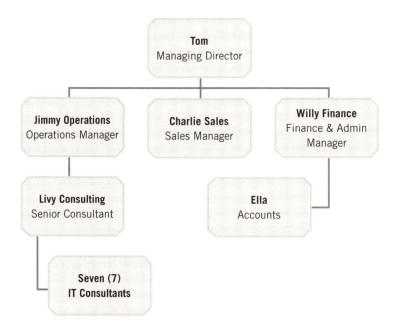

MISSION GOALS

Tom and I revisited the draft Mission Goals he'd set earlier on Io.

The Mission Goals for Dylan IT were:

1. **Business Performance**—Implementation of Mission Plan. Deliver Mission Goals. Tom/Jimmy

2. **Products and Services**—Review and develop products/services, pricing, and market. Jimmy

3. **Crew**—Develop, document, and implement individual Crew Goals. Livy

4. **Systems**—Develop, document, and implement business systems and processes. Willy

5. **Marketing and Sales**—Develop and implement a Marketing Plan and sales-based activities to communicate with niche market and hit revenue targets. Charlie

"Remember these Mission Goals, Tom?" I prompted.

"Sure do," said Tom.

CREW GOALS

"Well, think of these Mission Goals as a master list of business priorities. Imagine if all crew members had a list of their own individual Crew Goals and they were aligned to the overall business's Mission Goals. What if the crew's achievement of their Crew Goals were integrally linked to the achievement of the business's Mission Goals? What would that look like, Tom?"

"It would certainly reduce the current level of reliance on me, and I can see the synergies in the crew pulling together as a group to achieve our Mission Goals," Tom stated.

I took Tom through the concept of devising and documenting each individual's Crew Goals, noting that people find it hard to focus on more than three to five goals at once.

"The secret is to tell them the five most important goals you want them to focus on. They will be reviewed and rewarded based on their performance measured against these Crew Goals. Most crew members have a never-ending laundry list of things to do. With little or no guidance on how to prioritize this ever-growing list, crew members become overwhelmed and desensitized to executing tasks efficiently and effectively. When everything is urgent, nothing is urgent. Or alternatively, when every task is a priority, in reality there are no priorities."

Tom and I started to workshop the Crew Goals for each manager. While we tried to make these Crew Goals as objective as possible, we understood that some goals would be assessable only on a subjective basis.

"The aim is to ensure that the documented Crew Goals encapsulate 80% or more of the crew member's role," I said. "The Crew Goals should align with achieving the overall company's Mission Goals. Crew Goals must be clear and concise. Managers distribute Crew Goals to each crew member, explaining that their performance, remuneration, and rewards will hinge on these goals."

I recommended drafting the Crew Goals on one page with a title for the goal and a narrative explaining each goal.

Tom and I initially drafted Crew Goals for each of his four managers—Jimmy Operations, Livy Consulting, Charlie Sales, and Willy Finance.

This is what the managers' Crew Goals looked like (Note: The first two Crew Goals for Jimmy and the first Crew Goal for Livy, Charlie and Willy are also Mission Goals of Dylan IT):

Jimmy—Operations Manager: Crew Goals

1. **Business Performance**—Implementation of Mission Plan. Deliver Mission Goals.

2. **Products and Services**—Review and develop products/services, pricing, and niche market.

3. **Operational Management**—Accountability for the day-to-day operational running of Dylan IT. Responsibility for the management and overall performance of the management team: Livy, Charlie, and Willy.

4. **IT Consulting Team**—Drive, support, and manage Livy on the overall performance of the IT Consulting Team.

5. **Business Administration**—Accountability for ensuring all Crew Reviews and Mission Meetings are held with follow-up actions attended to. Responsibility for the business administration of Dylan IT. Complete MBA over next four years.

Livy—Senior Consultant: Crew Goals

1. **Crew Goals**—Develop, document, and implement individual Crew Goals.

2. **IT Consulting Team**—Accountability for operational management of the IT Consulting Team. Ensure Mission Meetings for IT Consulting Team are held and follow-up actions completed.

3. **Financial Performance of IT Consulting Team**—Accountable for meeting or exceeding revenue and gross profit targets for the IT Consulting Team.

4. **Crew Reviews**—Schedule and conduct Crew Reviews for IT Consulting Team.

5. **Professional and Personal Development**—Attend HR and management training course. Complete business degree.

Charlie—Sales Manager: Crew Goals

1. **Marketing and Sales**—Develop and implement a Marketing Plan and sales-based activities to communicate with niche market to hit sales/gross profit targets.

2. **Niche**—Follow niche market definition, transition out non-niche customers and create marketing content for multichannel communication.

3. **Customers**—Conduct customer stocktake with Tom. Implement customer care model to ensure all customers are "touched" on a periodic basis at the frequency agreed under the A, B, C, D, and E customer rating model.

4. **Sales-based Activity**—Schedule and conduct a minimum of five (5) meetings per week with niche customers and prospects (manufacturers and distributors).

5. **Complete marketing degree.**

Willy—Finance and Administration Manager: Crew Goals

1. **Systems**—Develop, document, and implement Dylan IT business processes.

2. **Dashboard Reporting**—Ensure monthly dashboard reporting for prior month is completed by Day 15 of each month. Complete dashboard reporting on a timely and accurate basis.

3. **Mission Meetings**—Be accountable for scheduling of weekly Finance and Business Admin Meetings, ensuring follow-up actions are completed. Schedule and conduct monthly Crew Review with Ella.

4. **Finance and Administration**—Overall accountability for the finance and administration function of Dylan IT. Direct report of Ella.

5. **Compliance and Governance**—Ensure that all compliance and governance requirements of Dylan IT are met.

"See how the Mission Goals are listed as the number one Crew Goal of each manager? That ensures that each manager's number one goal is directly linked to Dylan IT's Mission Goals," I summarized.

"I should also mention that your individual Crew Goals, Tom, are simply the Mission Goals of Dylan IT. So you don't get off the hook."

Tom smiled and nodded, acknowledging the fact that he as MD—Managing Director—and owner would be ultimately accountable for the business achieving its Mission Goals.

I continued. "We will provide the managers with management reports and extracts that show the budgeted targets, key metrics, and regular reporting. Willy Finance will help us in this area.

"Of course, we need to have Crew Goals set for all crew members, not just our managers. So you'll need to draft Crew Goals for the seven IT consultants and Ella in accounts. We can speak to Willy Finance later about drafting Ella's Crew Goals. But I think it's important to get Livy Consulting in to discuss drafting the Crew Goals for the IT consultants."

"Agreed, Darren. I'll go and get Livy now."

When Tom returned with her, we ran Livy through the link between

Dylan IT's Mission Goals and her individual Crew Goals. We further explained that Jimmy, Charlie, and Willy also had individual Crew Goals. We touched on the Crew Chart to help Livy understand her new role. The conversation then turned to her being responsible for driving the IT consultants' Crew Goals.

"How would you suggest I approach this?" Livy asked.

"Follow the same format as you see on your Crew Goals," I suggested. "Limit their goals to five. There might be four goals that relate specifically to their functional role. The fifth goal might relate to their professional and personal development."

"I see," said Livy.

"Try and make the top goals linked to delivering on their consulting role," Tom said. "We are implementing minimum chargeable hour requirements, we will be driving timesheets harder, and we want to institute weekly invoicing. All these things will be measured and reviewed. Their performance will be measured against this, and their remuneration and rewards will be linked to this."

"That sounds great," Livy said, nodding. "I'll use the template of my Crew Goals to document it for the seven IT consultants. Based on the Crew Chart you just showed me, should I get Jimmy to review this when I finish?"

"That would be perfect," Tom said encouragingly.

We asked Livy to leave us while we discussed remunerating and rewarding the team. Livy would rejoin us later to discuss Crew Reviews.

REMUNERATING AND REWARDING CREW

As Livy left the boardroom, Tom and I turned our attention to the next topic—crew pay.

Total Remuneration Package (TRP)

"The goal should be to set your remuneration levels at or above market. Ideally, above market," I said. "This can provide greater crew retention and competitive advantage." I discussed with Tom what I call the "controllables" and the "uncontrollables" in relation to remunerating and rewarding crew members.

"Paying at or above market salary is a controllable, because you can reduce the risk of a crew member leaving for pay reasons. To contrast, a crew member leaving because of family circumstances or a decision to live overseas are uncontrollable factors. The motto is: get the controllables right, and try to influence the uncontrollables as much as you can."

I asked Tom, "If I asked each crew member in your team what they earned, what would they say?"

"That's easy. Their base salary or their hourly rate," Tom stated emphatically.

"Is that right though?" I queried.

"Yes, how else would you calculate it?" Tom asked, sounding a little frustrated at having to explain the obvious.

"But that's not what you pay them," I said calmly.

"I'm not following you," Tom said, sensing he was missing something.

I explained that we had to reeducate our crew to understand their "Total Remuneration Package," or "TRP." The TRP includes their base salary, entitlements, benefits, and other rewards. If Livy is on $60,000 salary but she receives $10,000 in additional entitlements and is provided with a motor vehicle benefit of $15,000, she is on $85,000 ($60,000 + $10,000 + $15,000). It's critical that we always discuss Livy's TRP as $85,000 rather than the $60,000 base. Livy earns an $85,000 TRP, and this needs to be both understood and acknowledged when discussing her remuneration.

The penny had dropped for Tom; my explanation clicked for him.

"Now I get it," he said. "All this time I've been having pay discussions around base salary or hourly rate when I should have been talking about TRP, as you call it."

"That's okay," I comforted Tom. "Let's just make a commitment now that we always talk TRP when discussing pay."

Benefits

I took the explanation further. "Benefits are typically the additional items that employers provide to crew members over and above their salary or base hourly rate," I explained. "For simplicity, let's refer to benefits as non-salary items that are provided in kind. Ignoring the varying tax consequences of providing crew member benefits internationally, the notion of providing benefits to crew members can be a powerful tool in both rewarding and retaining key team members.

"The types of benefits provided to your crew members are limited only by your imagination. Subject to your budget and local taxation laws, providing benefits to your crew is a great way to empower individuals, make them feel valued, and really engage them. The more vanilla benefits may include providing company motor vehicles, health insurance, professional industry subscriptions, training, and other sweeteners."

Tom interrupted. "I always hear about companies offering additional benefits. What are some of those?"

"Less mainstream benefits," I said, "could be an extra week's holiday leave, time off in lieu of overtime worked, company gymnasiums, in-house dining, and handpicked gifts for milestone celebrations such as weddings.

"At the more exotic and creative end of providing benefits, these might include an annual 'company day' off, an in-house nap room, weekly in-house massage services, or a day off for your birthday."

"Hey, I'm getting a bit overwhelmed here," Tom said, leaning back in his chair.

"Then let's take a walk around," I said. "I need some fresh air myself."

Rewards

When we returned to the meeting room, I took up the topic of rewards.

"Rewards tend to be more specifically based on individual or team performance when measured against a project or goal. An individual or team could be provided with a non-monetary reward in the form of a fully paid holiday to an exotic location for completing a project successfully or for achieving a particular goal.

"Monetary rewards are often in the form of a dollar-based bonus or incentive being paid for the achievement of a goal. These are typically 'at risk' and are paid only if the target goal is achieved. A typical example of this is a Sales Manager's bonus for hitting a sales target."

I continued. "The use of rewards in remunerating individuals and teams can be very powerful. The use of incentives and rewards measured against achieving the business's Mission Goals creates a win-win focus for the three critical parties—individual, team, and organization. From a business owner's perspective, these monetized rewards are paid only if the goals and targets are achieved. They are funded out of success."

CREW REVIEWS, ANNUAL PERFORMANCE REVIEWS, AND ANNUAL REMUNERATION REVIEWS

We asked Livy Consulting to rejoin us so we could introduce her to the idea of holding a series of internal meetings between crew members and their managers to appraise their performance against their Crew Goals.

Crew Reviews

"So what are these Crew Reviews, Darren?" Livy asked inquisitively.

"A Crew Review, Livy, is a one-on-one session scheduled monthly in which crew members meet with direct reports on a more strategic level," I said. "Operational meetings and interaction are an important aspect of day-to-day business. However, the ability to create a forum through the monthly Crew Review to discuss each individual's Crew Goals and overall performance is invaluable.

"In these Crew Reviews, the direct report is able to appraise and provide feedback on the crew member's progress in relation to his Crew Goals. Together they can identify gaps and barriers that need to be removed in order to succeed. The crew member is able to draw on the experience of his direct report and get help in overcoming obstacles that are holding him back."

"How do we make sure Crew Reviews happen?" Livy asked.

"After issuing each individual crew member with their Crew Goals, you and the management team must be disciplined in scheduling and conducting Crew Reviews. While I'd recommend a monthly rolling format of Crew

Reviews for Dylan IT, Livy, some clients choose to conduct Crew Reviews quarterly or even six-monthly."

Annual Performance Reviews

I then went on to explain Annual Performance Reviews to Tom and Livy.

"The Annual Performance Review is a review of performance, not of remuneration. It is a more comprehensive version of the monthly Crew Reviews. The crew member's performance for the prior six months (the six-month period since the last Annual Remuneration Review) is appraised by the direct report. The crew member's progress on their Crew Goals is appraised, including a review of current projects and overall job performance. The parties note the observations and agreed issues for action over the six months ahead, leading up to the Annual Remuneration Review."

Annual Remuneration Reviews

I went on to describe the next type of assessment. "The Annual Remuneration Review is a review of both performance and remuneration. It is scheduled six months after the Annual Performance Review. The periodic scheduling of these reviews helps to manage crew member expectations and reduces random requests for increased remuneration outside of the scheduled planner. Further, it provides an annual forum for reviewing remuneration."

Livy asked, "Can you clarify the distinction between agendas in the Annual Performance Review and those of the Annual Remuneration Review?"

I responded, "The agenda for the Annual Remuneration Review is the same as the Annual Performance Review, with the additional agenda item of conducting a review of the crew member's remuneration. The remuneration should be considered and assessed as a Total Remuneration Package (TRP) inclusive of base salary, employee entitlements, and benefits.

"Each crew member, in conjunction with their direct reports, should have Crew Reviews, Annual Performance Reviews, and Annual Remuneration Reviews scheduled in their diaries. The scheduling of these in advance creates a discipline of ensuring these important meetings are held." I handed them my proposed calendar of these dates.

Mission Management Calendar

Manager	Crew Reviews (monthly)	Annual Performance Reviews (mid-year)	Annual Remuneration Reviews (end-of-year)
Tom	Jimmy Charlie Willy	Jimmy Charlie Willy Livy	Jimmy Charlie Willy Livy IT Consultants (7) Ella
Jimmy	Livy	Livy	Livy IT Consultants (7)
Livy	IT Consultants (7)	IT Consultants (7)	IT Consultants (7)
Charlie	n/a	n/a	n/a
Willy	Ella	Ella	Ella

Tom and Livy had been listening intently and thinking deeply about the proposed changes to the team at Dylan IT.

"We'll need your help in setting this all up and managing the team if we're going to make these changes, Darren. We'll also need some help in creating new ways to reward the crew," Tom concluded.

"Absolutely, Tom," I said. "That's what we need to focus on at our next meeting. But rest assured, managing the team is about to get a whole lot easier for you."

MISSION LOG

Crew: Mission Management

- Tom reviews the Organizational Chart, which is now referred to as the Crew Chart, agreeing to change its structure to reduce the day-to-day operational reliance on him.

- Tom and I revisit the Mission Goals, affirming them for the mission.

- I introduce Crew Goals, which are the top five goals of each individual crew member. The achievement of these Crew Goals leads to the achievement of Mission Goals.

- Tom learns that each of the Dylan IT Mission Goals is the top Crew Goal of each manager.

- Tom drafts Crew Goals for Jimmy, Livy, Charlie, and Willy.

- Tom meets with Livy to brief her on drafting Crew Goals for each individual IT consultant.

- Tom learns the importance of assessing crew remuneration as a Total Remuneration Package (TRP).

- Livy and Tom learn that Crew Reviews are monthly, one-on-one sessions held between a crew member and his/her direct report.

- Livy and Tom learn of Annual Performance Reviews, which are reviews of a crew member's performance, *not* remuneration.

- Livy and Tom learn of Annual Remuneration Reviews, which are reviews of a crew member's performance *and* remuneration.

- Tom, Livy, and I develop a Mission Management Calendar to schedule these reviews.

CHAPTER 10

Mission Meetings:
Operational Functionality

Tom and I had arranged to meet up and talk about management. I sensed that Tom didn't truly believe that he had a management team yet, so I wanted to drive the power of a management team home to him.

"Remember last session when we restructured your Organizational Chart into the Crew Chart?" I said.

He nodded.

"The big shift in drafting the Crew Chart," I continued, "is that you now have only three individuals reporting to you directly—Jimmy, Charlie, and Willy. In the original Organizational Chart, you had all twelve individual team members reporting to you.

"Jimmy as Operations Manager now oversees operations. He will be responsible for project management, operational customer relationship management, and crew. Livy will report to Jimmy and fulfill the position of Senior Consultant. Livy will be responsible for time, cost, and quality in relation to the entire team of seven IT consultants. The consulting team will directly report to Livy."

"I'm with you. Keep going," Tom encouraged, not wanting to interrupt the flow of this logic.

"Charlie as Sales Manager still reports directly to you. The two of you need to work closely on your niche market and the Marketing Plan. Charlie would also work in tandem with Jimmy on new customers to ensure a smooth transition into operations.

"And then there's Willy as Finance and Admin Manager reporting directly to you. Willy needs to provide you with up-to-date cash flows, finance information, and management reporting. He'll also update you on payroll and personnel matters. Ella in accounts will report directly to Willy. Willy will interact with Jimmy, Livy, and Charlie in supporting the administrative requirements of the business."

"So what will I do?" Tom joked.

"We'll get to you later," I said, smiling at Tom.

"So under the Crew Chart, I have only three direct reports, rather than twelve. Jimmy and Livy will take up much of the operational load, which will free me up. Willy will oversee Ella. My four managers—Jimmy, Livy, Charlie, and Willy—will work more closely together to run operations, service customers, and support me in running the business."

"Sounds good, doesn't it, Tom?" I encouraged.

For the first time since starting the business, Tom could see a way to break free of the rut he'd been stuck in for years. Finally he'd have more time to work on the business strategically and be a business owner rather than a business operator. His mind raced, imagining the possibilities.

"Now let's figure out how to do it," I suggested. "That is, how the management team will implement operational functionality throughout Dylan IT.

"But first, let's talk about informal management techniques. Second, we'll move on to formal management techniques through the use of Mission Meetings."

INFORMAL MANAGEMENT OF CREW

"What I'm about to outline is an approach to informal management that we'll need to teach Jimmy, Livy, and Willy. They have crew members directly reporting to them now, so this will help them manage effectively," I explained.

Informal management refers to the day-to-day, unstructured supervision and management of individuals and the team. There are five key areas that I suggested the management team focus on here:

- Open-door policy
- Set windows of allocated time
- Laps
- Mini check-ins
- Project-specific interactions

"Firstly, the 'open-door policy' is often misunderstood. The idea of managers having their door open and providing available access for team members to speak with them is great in principle, but not quite so good in practice. This policy came about from the observation that management had been considered unapproachable and unavailable by team members trying to access them. The open-door policy is a great concept when implemented correctly. In many instances, this policy was implemented on the basis of the manager's door being open almost permanently. This often led to constant interruption, resulting in a manager failing to keep pace with her workload. My attitude toward the open-door policy is to use the door like a motel vacancy sign. If a manager is working on a strategic matter or speaking with somebody confidentially in person or on the phone, she should close her door, which indicates 'don't interrupt me.' Alternatively, if the manager is working on general operational or administrative matters, then the door can be left open, signaling, 'I'm available for discussion.'

"Secondly," I continued, "an effective informal management tool is the setting of standard, scheduled windows of time where a manager is available. For example, a manager might schedule from 3 PM to 5 PM on Tuesdays and Thursdays as standing, open windows of contact for individuals. Crew members know that these standing windows are open for contact with their manager, so they can plan and prepare their queries in readiness for these. Further, these windows allow spontaneous access to the manager on those days.

"Thirdly, the technique I refer to as 'doing laps' is noteworthy. A business owner I coached asked me to help him make the transition from working in a technical role to acting in the role of General Manager. He asked me what the best General Managers I'd seen had done to set them apart. I recalled a successful General Manager once told me it was all about 'doing laps.' He explained that he did regular laps, or circuits, on foot, through operational work areas to ensure he spoke to all individuals at least once per day. He would do his laps on a regular and disciplined basis first thing in the morning, mid-morning, after lunch, and late afternoon. In doing so, he explained, he had his finger on the pulse of operations and was given great insight into issues and problems in real time. Further, it influenced productivity, morale, and engagement because senior management members were seen on the floor and interacted with every crew member.

"Fourthly, mini check-ins refer to rolling contact with individual crew members or project teams to update status and remove any hurdles or obstacles that may be blocking their progress. For junior crew, these may be as often as daily. For intermediate crew, rolling check-ins every forty-eight hours on Mondays, Wednesdays, and Fridays can be used. Weekly check-ins can be used effectively for senior crew or project teams.

"Finally, managers might also allocate specific time for the informal management of projects. These meetings may be with specific individuals working on the project, or the entire project team. The frequency, content, and venue for managing projects will vary on a case-by-case basis."

Tom and I agreed to meet with Jimmy, Livy, and Willy to expand on these informal management tools. This would immediately help them manage their team effectively and efficiently. Tom committed to using these techniques himself in managing Jimmy, Willy, and Charlie.

MISSION MEETINGS

"I now want to introduce you to formal management techniques," I said. "Let's call these Mission Meetings, Tom. These Mission Meetings will be the glue that keeps all the strategy we developed on Io connected and alive."

But Tom protested. "You know I'm not big on meetings, Darren."

I pushed back. "These are not meetings for the sake of meetings. Just a few highly targeted meetings of different crew members. These rolling meetings must become part of the culture of Dylan IT. They need to be nonnegotiable and run like clockwork."

"So take me through what you're proposing for these Mission Meetings," Tom invited.

Weekly Mission Meetings

"I suggest we implement four weekly meetings," I said.

"The Crew Operations Meeting is the cornerstone of every thriving business. Operations meetings require all crew members to attend. Weekly operations meetings are best done early in the week on either Monday morning or Tuesday morning. The meeting must have a standard agenda with a focus on operational matters. Tom, you could chair the meeting, with each of the four managers having a departmental agenda item. A rotating scribe (a different crew member each week) is appointed to take down meeting notes of agreed actions. The scribe must email the agreed actions to each team member by close of business on the meeting day."

I had learned from my other clients that the key to successful operations meetings is to keep them short, sharp, and to the point. The content of the meeting must be kept strictly to operational issues only. Outside discussion between specific staff members, broader discussion of strategic issues, or business administration matters must be short-circuited and taken offline. This is primarily the role of the Chair, but any individual can call this. It's not that these topics are unimportant, but rather that they need to be discussed at a separate time outside the operations meeting. The operations meeting agenda needs to be followed in a disciplined manner, with a strict adherence to operational matters.

"Okay," Tom agreed. "I can see the benefit of the entire crew meeting up weekly on operational matters."

"The second weekly meeting could be with the IT Consulting Team—the IT Operations Meeting. After getting input from the entire crew at the Crew Operations Meeting, Jimmy would meet with Livy and the other IT consultants for a specific team meeting in relation to operational matters including project status, work-in-progress, technical issues, timesheets, billing, and customer matters. Jimmy or Livy would chair this meeting."

Tom got it. "The IT Consulting Team must communicate more frequently and across all current projects. Go on, Darren."

"Now we get to the third weekly meeting, which could be a Finance and Business Admin Meeting. This meeting would be attended by Jimmy, Willy, and you, Tom. This meeting would relate specifically to cash flow, banking and finance, management reporting, and general commercial issues.

"And then finally the fourth weekly meeting could be a Sales Meeting. This meeting would be attended by Charlie, Jimmy, and you again, Tom. This would include customer review, customer/prospect meetings held, prospect pipeline, new customers, departing non-niche customer transition, and niche review.

"So that's it for the weekly meetings, Tom. When would be the best time to schedule these?" I asked.

"I'd say 8 AM Tuesdays for the Crew Operations Meeting. The IT Operations Meeting could follow that immediately at 9 AM on Tuesdays. I'd rather have the crew deployed on Mondays; get the week started with customers, and then come in early Tuesdays for these meetings. For the Finance and Business Admin Meeting, why don't we do that at 9 AM on Wednesday mornings, followed by the Sales Meeting at 10?" Tom suggested.

"Sounds great, Tom. Well done," I said. "And on a monthly basis, I suggest you implement a Management Team Meeting."

Monthly Mission Meetings

We agreed that the Management Team Meeting would be held monthly to review the progress on the business's Mission Goals, managers' key priorities within their individual Crew Goals, crew and crew member performance, stakeholder issues, and other commercial issues. Jimmy, Livy, Charlie, and Willy would attend and be responsible for presenting on their area of the business. This would include dashboard reporting issued by Willy.

The management team would agree on issues that need to be communicated with crew and would table these in the next weekly Crew Operations Meeting.

Quarterly Mission Meetings

"And finally, you should hold a Quarterly Crew Meeting with all crew members attending," I suggested to Tom.

"Quarterly Crew Meetings are very different from the weekly operational meetings. Quarterly Crew Meetings have a much different focus. These meetings have a more strategic rather than operational focus. The agenda might include areas such as prior quarter results, customer updates, key projects, departmental reporting, human resources, and business administration.

"Business performance measured against Mission Goals and targets would be reviewed. Of course, identifying what has to happen strategically within the business for the quarter ahead should also be discussed. These meetings could be chaired by Jimmy or Willy, with meeting notes circulated to all crew by email."

———————

"So that's it, Tom. Just four weekly meetings, one monthly meeting, and one quarterly meeting. That's a commitment of just four hours a week, normally. Even if we include the monthly and quarterly meetings, this equates to four and a half hours or half a day per week to run your business internally. That's just two days per month out of, say, twenty-two working days. Not bad, eh?"

"When you put it like that, Darren, it doesn't seem too overbearing, does it? If we can't commit to that, we're not taking this seriously," Tom stated.

"Are you willing to commit to this regime of Mission Meetings, Tom?"

"Yeah, I think I am," Tom said. "As long as they are run properly and actioned."

"We'll make sure they are, Tom," I assured.

This is what the table of Mission Meetings looked like:

Mission Meeting Calendar

Mission Meeting	Attendees	Scheduling
Crew Operations Meeting	ALL	8 AM Tuesdays
IT Operations Meeting	Jimmy, Livy, and IT consultants	9 AM Tuesdays
Finance and Business Admin Meeting	Tom, Jimmy, and Willy	9 AM Wednesdays
Sales Meeting	Tom, Charlie, and Jimmy	10 AM Wednesdays
Management Team Meeting	Tom, Jimmy, Livy, Charlie, and Willy	3rd Wednesday monthly at 11 AM
Quarterly Crew Meeting	ALL	3rd Tuesday after quarter-end at 10 AM

MANAGEMENT STYLE

Tom had a question for me. "I know we've established the members of the management team, the informal management techniques, and the formal management techniques through Mission Meetings. But what overarching role should I try and get the management team to play, Darren?"

"That's an interesting question, Tom. Remember when you drafted the Mission Plan and mapped out your vision through setting your Mission Goals? Well, the role of management is to control and direct the team to achieve this vision—basically, to deliver the results. At the macro business level, you have established your Mission Goals. At the micro level, you and the management team have established the Crew Goals for each individual crew member. With management driving each person to deliver on their Crew Goals, this creates a powerful alignment that flows on to the achievement of the company's Mission Goals. There is a synergy that exists between the individual and the business here. These priorities are not mutually exclusive, but are in fact correlated.

"The role of management is part art and part science," I went on. "The Mission Goals and the Crew Goals are the science. The art of management is engaging crew members and getting them committed to the mission. Engagement is based on an authentic connection and desire to do what's required to achieve the goal. It's a psychological buy-in from the crew member. Once a manager has engagement, she can then tackle empowerment. Empowerment is the art of making crew members believe they have the permission, ability, and resources to deliver on their goals. Engaging and empowering people is what it's all about."

"That makes sense," Tom said, rubbing his chin. "So they've got to control and manage resources to achieve the vision. Managers do this by engaging and empowering the team. But different management styles must influence this too."

"You're absolutely right, Tom. Different management styles get different results. The best managers I've seen have a collaborative and consultative approach. They believe in searching for the right mix of both internal and external input. They have an inclusive approach to getting the right answers. They have a humility that allows them to not care who comes up with the answer, as long as it's a right answer. And by the way, they have no problem with recognizing and rewarding individuals who deliver results. They know they're the real heroes. Great managers are also flexible, helpful, and supportive. They take a great interest in the individual, and know when to get in the trenches with crew members and when to step back. All these soft skills are rounded out with a generous dollop of humor."

I asked cautiously, "So how do you feel, Tom?"

He leaned back in his chair. "Excited, but still a bit scared and overwhelmed."

"The good news," I said, "is that our initial visit to the First Moon is over. We're leaving Io, the First Moon. While on Io, you set your strategy with integrity, authenticity, and deep consideration. I applaud you for having the courage to make these important changes. You've been able to leave your ego in the bottom drawer and assess your business future objectively and with humility. Well done."

Tom smiled proudly. "Let's have a beer, Darren, to celebrate and acknowl-edge our time on Io. I want to recognize this moment before we embark on our journey to the Second Moon."

"Can't argue with that invitation," I said, laughing. "We're off to the Second Moon—Europa."

With that, Tom disappeared into the boardroom to raid the fridge.

MISSION LOG

Mission Meetings: Operational Functionality

- Tom learns a range of informal management techniques.

- I introduce Tom to Mission Meetings. These important internal meet-ings are the glue that keeps strategy connected and alive within the organization.

- Tom introduces four weekly Mission Meetings, which are the Crew Operations Meeting, IT Operations Meeting, Finance and Business Admin Meeting, and Sales Meeting.

- Dylan IT introduces a Management Team Meeting scheduled to occur on a monthly basis.

- Dylan IT introduces a Quarterly Crew Meeting.

- Tom commits to adopting Mission Meetings within Dylan IT.

- Dylan IT adopts a Mission Meeting Calendar.

THE SECOND MOON: IMPLEMENTATION

By denying scientific principles,
one may maintain any paradox.

—Galileo Galilei

CHAPTER 11

Mission Plan:
Implementing Strategy

Can you imagine the moment? The moment Galileo discovered Jupiter's moons? You know that feeling of euphoria when your heart rises and seems to lift you up? It feels like you're walking on air with your head in the clouds. Yes—that one!

We feel it when we fall in love. We can feel it through a sports victory. A particular song at a live concert. Or perhaps our wedding day. The moment our child is born. It could even be the applause of an audience after a performance we've given.

Way back in the seventeenth century, Galileo must have experienced one of these heartfelt moments of pure joy and ecstasy. This is how he relates his first unknowing glimpse of Jupiter's moons:

> At the outset I thought them to be fixed stars, as I have said.
> But returning to the same investigation—led by what, I
> do not know—I found a very different arrangement.

Those seven words, "led by what, I do not know," overturned centuries of human belief. The long-held popular belief that the planets revolved around the earth was suddenly dead. I admire the humility in Galileo's seven words. It shows an innate curiosity and a thirst for greater understanding. It almost suggests Galileo was not so much asking why, but why not . . . simply because he could.

Sitting up late at night all by himself, the magnitude of his discovery—and the realization this would change the world forever—must have been surreal.

This is exactly why you must revisit your strategy. There is no point looking through the same lens using the same paradigm and belief system. You'll simply see the same picture again. You need to take a different lens—a more powerful lens—to look at your strategy objectively and creatively in ways you'd never imagined. Like Galileo, you may say to yourself, "I am led by what I do not know." Tom's discoveries on the First Moon were going to change his world forever. With his own metaphorical telescope, Tom had studied the First Moon and its landscape. The landscape on the First Moon was significantly different from that of Tom's earthly business paradigm. There was a systematic and logical geography to the First Moon that changed his perspective completely.

One of the many joys of my work is that I have the opportunity to observe the belief structures of business owners and to garner insights every day. It amazes me how often I hear a business owner react defensively when presented with a new perspective, effectively closing down the opportunity to explore a better process or a proposed solution to a nagging problem. The respondents may say they've read about it, heard about it, went to a seminar about it. They know it. Yet my observational response is always the same . . . "knowing isn't doing."

Just think about this for a moment. How many times have you been guilty of being offered an insight, resource, or solution to a problem, only to say, "Yeah, I know about that"?

The reason I say "knowing isn't doing" is because there is no point knowing something if you don't act on it. What's the point of knowing about workplace discrimination if you don't have a policy regarding it? Or knowing about computer backup procedures without using them? You know about time-management techniques, yet you allow your working day to randomly play out without any structure. It's just plain crazy, yet so many business owners do this.

Tom had called me prior to our meeting today to share his anticipation at embarking on his initial visit to the Second Moon. I, too, was keen to get started on this important next stage of his business journey.

I picked up Tom from his office and we headed out for a coffee meeting. I had strategically chosen a café overlooking the bay. The sea was calm and the water shone like a sheet of glass. Taking a table outside by the water, we got down to Second Moon discussions. "Tom," I began, "let's imagine that this café is located on Europa itself. Remember I previously explained that Europa is smooth and fluid?"

Two coffees from the Europa café promptly arrived.

"There's lots of water out there, Tom," I said, pointing toward the water.

"And so smooth," Tom observed.

"With so much water on Europa, you want it to be smooth and calm. Implementing your strategy needs to be done not only methodically, but also fluidly. The fluidity of Europa provides the flexibility required to implement your strategy—your Mission Plan. You rarely will implement your Mission Plan smoothly the first time. It will require trial and error and constant corrections to have it implemented comprehensively throughout Dylan IT."

"Why is trial and error involved?" Tom protested. "Can't we just implement the Mission Plan and get it right the first time?"

"Maybe. Maybe not. It's like new habits, Tom. They don't always stick on the first go."

Tom softened. "I guess you're right, Darren." He sipped his coffee as I spoke.

"Think of it this way, Tom. You and the Dylan IT crew have been doing things the same way for years. Now I've come along and challenged you and the crew to change your mode of operation. Don't you think you might need a few attempts to start operating in a different way?"

"Okay," Tom said. "When you explain it like that, I get you."

"Remember your friend Galileo, Tom? Second Moon thinking requires buckets of patience. Old habits die hard. New habits require patience and sensitivity in being implemented."

"Ah," Tom said with a nod, "patience. You told me to carry Galileo's attitudes in my pocket. You're right. Patience was one of them. I will remember that on Europa."

"So, Tom . . . Second Moon thinking while on Europa. Focus on implementation. Smooth and fluid. Patience."

"Okay. That will be my mantra," Tom said. He smiled out at the water.

I reviewed the recent Profit & Loss statements that Tom had brought along. I suggested he change his reporting format to include all the direct costs—such as IT consulting wages and materials (hardware and software) in a "cost of sales" section at the top of the Profit & Loss. We could then deduct these direct costs of sale from our sales revenue to arrive at a gross profit. The gross profit is the profit made after direct costs of sale but before general overhead expenses. Overhead expenses include items such as telephone, rent, and office wages that generally don't vary based on sales turnover.

We then analyzed the Profit & Loss statement for the last financial year, and found the following:

Sales Revenue	**$2,500,000**
Direct Costs (IT consulting wages including Jimmy/Livy and materials)	($1,750,000)
Gross Profit	**$750,000 (30%)**
Indirect wages (Willy, Ella, Charlie, Tom)	($375,000)
General overhead expenses	($200,000)
Net Operating Profit	**$175,000 (7% shareholder return)**

Tom's jaw dropped. "Is that all we made?"

While not totally disastrous, it wasn't a pretty picture. Tom took some solace that his salary of $125,000, when added to the net operating profit of $175,000, meant he and Sarah had earned $300,000 last year. However, the shareholder return of 7% as investor wasn't great, and Tom's current salary of $125,000 was below market rates for his operational employee contribution as Managing Director.

We had to get the operating profit margin above 10% and ideally towards 15% and beyond. I felt this was possible in the new market niche.

"Even though the shareholders of Dylan IT are you and Sarah, it is still important to analyze the shareholder return on an arm's-length basis. If the shareholders were third parties, they would assess the 7% return seriously and question whether or not this was a good rate of return. You and Sarah both need to wear your shareholder hats when assessing the shareholder return from the business. Given the business is your most significant asset outside of the family home, I'd like to see the shareholder return closer to 15% as a minimum, based on your industry."

"I understand, Darren," Tom said. "I like the idea of separating the salary I receive for my operational contribution from the investment return Sarah and I receive as shareholders."

I finished my coffee. "That's right," I said. "They are totally different income streams and must be recognized and analyzed as such."

I now wanted to get Tom to experience a business owner's eagle-eye view of where the business should target itself overall—on a macro level. I'd seen his jaw drop when we reviewed last financial year's operating profit of $175,000, so I felt we should now draft an overall budget target for the new financial year. Charlie would have input on the sales mix and his personal targets.

Tom felt that the new products, increased chargeable/recoverable hours, and the higher hourly charge-out rates would increase sales revenue by at least 20%. I suggested that the gross profit would also increase from 30% to at least 36% as a result of these combined factors. I recommended Tom increase his salary as Managing Director from $125,000 to $150,000 for the new financial year. It was still below market, but closer to a true evaluation of Tom's operational role in the organization.

I suggested Tom consider Jimmy Operations receiving a $20,000 increase to his Total Remuneration Package (TRP) to reflect his new role of Operations Manager. Livy Consulting, Charlie Sales, and Willy Finance could receive a $10,000 increase to their TRPs. I introduced the idea that the managers could participate in an incentive scheme in future years financed by increased profits.

I felt we should address salaries and rewards for other crew based on their performance and the company's performance over the next financial year. Tom agreed.

Tom and I put together a Profit & Loss budget for the next year.

Here's how last year's actual Profit & Loss compared with next year's budgeted Profit & Loss:

	Actual Last Year	Budget Next Year
Sales Turnover	$2,500,000	$3,000,000
Direct Costs (IT consulting wages includ- ing Jimmy/Livy and materials)	($1,750,000)	($1,920,000)
Gross Profit	$750,000 (30%)	$1,080,000 (36%)
Indirect wages (Willy, Ella, Charlie, Tom)	($375,000)	($420,000)
General overhead expenses	($200,000)	($210,000)
Net Operating Profit	$175,000 (7%)	$450,000 (15%)
Add Tom's salary back	($125,000)	($150,000)
Total Return (Shareholder and operational return combined)	$300,000	$600,000

Tom's eyes widened when he realized that he could potentially double his Total Return (combined shareholder and operational return) in twelve months.

We agreed that the analysis we'd done on budgeting would form the nucleus of our targets for the financial year ahead. I explained to Tom that while on Europa we would put together some more specific numbers around the Mission Plan, in addition to creating a new budget for future years. It was important that we include the managers in these discussions.

We next asked Jimmy Operations to join us. After all, Jimmy would be accountable with Tom for implementing the Mission Plan, delivering on Mission Goals, and reengineering Dylan IT products and services.

We briefed Jimmy Operations on the target sales revenue, gross profit, and net operating profit for the financial year ahead. He understood the logic and the need to set higher revenue targets.

We then introduced the Mission Goal in relation to products and services. Mission Goal #2 was to review and develop Dylan IT's products, services, pricing, and market, so we also asked Charlie Sales to join Jimmy Operations, Tom, and me.

"We've got you two guys in here," Tom started, "because you will be implementing our Mission Plan—Jimmy in products and services, and Charlie in marketing and sales."

Tom went on, "Jimmy, you'll be helping us implement a new offering of products and services, priced at new rates and targeted at our niche—manufacturers and distributors. Over the next twelve months, we want to transition to exclusively servicing this sector."

Jimmy scowled. "What about our other customers that aren't manufacturers and distributors?" he asked.

"Charlie and I will migrate them out over time," Tom said. "We have completed a comprehensive customer stocktake classifying customers as A, B, C, D, or E. Over time, we want only A and B customers from the manufacturing and distribution sector."

"Okay," Jimmy said slowly. "And how do we replace the revenue lost from specializing in this narrower niche?"

"Great question, Jimmy," Tom enthused, "we're getting to that."

We reviewed the proprietary software that Dylan IT provided to customers at virtually no margin. Everyone agreed that we could simply brand the software under the Dylan IT name and sell it exclusively to manufacturers and distributors.

"There are fundamentally three types of software sold, based on modules surrounding customer relationship management databases, inventory management, and point-of-sale," Tom suggested.

"What price points would you suggest, Tom?" I asked.

"The basic could be $1,500; the intermediate, $3,000; and the fully integrated, say, $6,000," Tom mused.

"How do you feel about selling the software at that price, Charlie?" I asked.

"I think that could work," Charlie said.

Jimmy added, "I think the real kicker to that, guys, is in adding compulsory service-level agreements."

"How would that work, Jimmy?" I asked.

"I think we need to lock in an annual commitment from our customers," Jimmy said. "If we are going to specialize in their niche, and offer niche-specific proprietary software, then we need to get paid appropriately to look after them well, as true experts in their sector."

"Go on," Tom encouraged.

"Well, I think we could charge something like $6,000, $12,000, and $18,000 respectively each year for supporting the three software programs. The three service-level agreements (SLAs) would state specifically what is included. Consulting, customization, and other customer-centric work would be charged in addition to the SLA fee."

Charlie added, "The SLA fees could be charged quarterly in advance, via direct debit. This would eliminate debtors and chasing money."

"That would really help Willy with invoicing and cash flow," Tom said, "not to mention profitability."

"So is this the direction we are taking?" I asked. "The three software programs and the corresponding SLAs will now represent six products sold to our niche market of manufacturers and distributors?"

Everyone agreed this was a game changer.

Jimmy Operations revisited our earlier discussions on pricing. Average hourly rates would be increased by $10 per hour. Jimmy, with Livy Consulting's help, would focus on increasing chargeable hours, up from the appalling current rate of just 50% to 75% over the next twelve months. Over time, this could be higher with the additional efficiencies realized from the three SLAs.

Charlie Sales then revisited the Marketing Plan and outlined the work that needed to be done for the blog, website upgrade, brochure, articles, video, and social networking. Given Charlie's workload in regard to developing content for the Marketing Plan, Tom and Charlie agreed that Charlie would attend one meeting per day, or five per week, with customers and prospects. Initially, this would be sufficient in Dylan IT's new and narrower niche.

Tom, Jimmy, and I agreed to support Charlie in creating niche-centric recyclable content.

We agreed to update the Mission Plan for the target sales revenue and other metrics. The Mission Goals would be updated also.

In wrapping up the meeting, we noted the need to meet up together again with Livy Consulting and Willy Finance. They too would be impacted by the introduction of new products and by the decision to specialize in a narrower niche. Their contribution to the reengineering of Dylan IT would also be pivotal in synergizing operations.

Leaving the boardroom, I left Tom, Jimmy, and Charlie to continue animated discussions around the journey Dylan IT was embarking upon.

Implementation on Europa had commenced.

MISSION LOG

Mission Plan: Implementing Strategy

- Tom realizes that knowing isn't doing and that Second Moon thinking drives implementation.

- Tom accepts that strategy is rarely implemented seamlessly on a first attempt.

- Tom learns that Mission Meetings are the glue that keeps the strategy on Io (the First Moon) alive within the organization.

- Tom agrees to increase the Total Remuneration Package (TRP) of each manager to reflect the increased responsibilities and accountabilities they have taken on.

- We agree the TRP of the wider crew, being the IT consultants and Ella, will be reviewed based on their performance over the next financial year.

- Tom, Jimmy Operations, and Charlie Sales agree to introduce three new software programs to be sold for $1,500, $3,000, and $6,000.

- Tom, Jimmy Operations, and Charlie Sales agree to introduce three new compulsory service-level-agreement (SLA) products to be sold for $6,000, $12,000, and $18,000.

- Tom increases hourly consulting charge-out rates immediately by $10 per hour.

- Tom commits to focus on productivity gains through increasing the chargeable hours of the IT consultants from 50% to 75%.

CHAPTER 12

Niche Me Up, Scotty

Second Moon thinking had really caught fire within Dylan IT.

Our most recent meeting with Jimmy Operations and Charlie Sales had gone exceptionally well. The discussion had led to the conceptualization of six new products: the three software programs and the three accompanying service-level agreements (SLAs). Jimmy and Charlie had bonded and had already met up twice together with Tom to scope out the reengineering of Dylan IT.

Now it was time to include Livy Consulting and Willy Finance in these discussions. With the entire management team of Tom, Jimmy, Livy, Charlie, and Willy in the boardroom, we got down to further implementation work.

Tom kicked off.

"Well, I know we haven't met up together as a group on this, but you're all aware we're changing tactics within the business.

"You're all part of the Dylan IT management team officially now, with Jimmy as Operations Manager, Livy as Senior Consultant, Charlie as Sales Manager, and of course Willy as Finance and Admin Manager."

A few nervous smiles were exchanged around the room.

"To manage your expectations, I'll meet up with you individually over the next fortnight to explain your new roles in greater detail. Following that, we will hold a Crew Launch at an external venue to explain the new strategy for Dylan IT."

Tom went on to explain that the Mission Plan would set the strategy for the financial year ahead. The Mission Plan included the Mission Goals, which outlined the top five priorities for Dylan IT to achieve.

All managers would have their own Crew Goals, listing the top five priorities for which they were to be accountable. Livy had created Crew Goals for each of the seven IT consultants, while Willy Finance had created Crew Goals for Ella in accounts.

Tom paused and repeated that a more comprehensive explanation of this would be conducted through individual meetings with managers, a Management Team Launch, and a Crew Launch. In the meantime, Tom returned to the topic of explaining the interrelationship within the management team and how that would contribute to Dylan IT transitioning the business into its narrower niche market.

"Jimmy will be jointly responsible with me for delivering on the Mission Plan. However, more specifically, Jimmy will be rolling out a number of products under the Dylan IT brand. Over the next twelve to eighteen months, we aim to exclusively service the manufacturing and distribution sector," Tom stated.

"How will this affect the IT Consulting Team?" Livy gasped.

"It's okay, Liv," Jimmy offered. "We are introducing three software programs. They will be the basic, intermediate, and advanced versions we currently use for manufacturers and distributors. They'll be priced at $1,500, $3,000, and $6,000. Manufacturers and distributors currently represent just under 40% of Dylan IT's sales revenue. There will be a new revenue stream from the new products offered in our three software programs. The software product price is a one-time deal. However, an additional new revenue stream will come from the compulsory service-level agreements, or SLAs, for each of the software programs. The three SLAs will be billed quarterly at an annual fee of $6,000, $12,000, and $18,000. These are, of course, recurring each year, and we will treat them internally as products."

"What do we do with outsiders, those outside our manufacturing and distribution niche?" asked Livy.

Tom spoke next. "I think we need a specific plan and timeline for this so that there is a clear direction for all of us to follow. What if we did this? We have broken our customers into categories A to E. The E's will be notified that we can no longer service them. The C's and D's that are outsiders will be notified in six months that we will no longer be able to service them. We will offer a six-month transitional period of service after this notification to allow them to source another IT provider. Of the A's and B's, there is only one customer that is an outsider—my oldest client, Bill—and all of us agree that we wish to continue servicing him as an exception. So that cleans up our customer base, with only the C and D manufacturers and distributors left, which we need to work on making into A and B customers. And of course, from now on we accept only new customers that operate in the Australian Manufacturing and Distribution Sector. Sound reasonable?"

Everyone nodded.

"Won't people get upset with us if we won't service them?" Livy asked.

"Not if we do it with dignity and stealth," said Tom in a measured tone. "We'll give them sufficient time to make other arrangements, and we won't leave them in the lurch. We will transition them out over the next six to twelve months. I agree we need to do this in the right way. But I have confidence in you all as a management team, and I'll take any heat that comes of it."

"Thanks, Tom. I feel better hearing you explain it that way," said Livy.

"And how will we track the time spent working under the SLAs?" Willy Finance interjected.

"We will include specific support tasks under each SLA. Livy will ensure that the IT consultants charge their time by customer SLA. Each quarter, we will compare the quarterly SLA fee against the time recorded internally to that customer's SLA. We will monitor variances, and aim for over-recoveries," Tom stated.

"Will it be clear to customers what is and isn't included under the SLA?" Livy inquired.

"It will be crystal clear. The scope will be documented in the SLA issued to customers," Tom confirmed.

"There will be other revenue gains in the future for the business beyond these new products," Jimmy added.

"What are they?" Livy and Willy chimed in simultaneously.

"We've decided to increase hourly charge-out rates for the IT consultants by $10 per hour immediately," Tom said. "More will follow once we transition the business into the manufacturing and distribution sector more fully. But Livy will be driving productivity of the IT consultants, with a focus on increasing chargeable hours and recovered work hours from 50% to 75%."

He added, "With Livy managing the IT Consulting Team, Willy, you'll be developing and documenting the Dylan IT business systems. The systematization of business processes will add efficiency gains throughout the entire organization."

"And returning back to the question of how we transition to exclusively servicing the manufacturing and distribution sector," I added, "Charlie is developing a comprehensive Marketing Plan supported by sales-based activity to strengthen existing manufacturing and distribution customer relationships, as well as targeting new niche customers."

"We will need to work together closely," Tom said, "to manage the transition into our manufacturing and distribution niche. Charlie and Jimmy will collaborate on this with me. We'll need to communicate internally on how we transition the non-niche customers out of the business."

Tom and I outlined the Mission Meetings with the management team. We agreed to table these in the Crew Launch.

"And I don't get off easy either. I commit to supporting all of you in achieving your individual Crew Goals, which will, in turn, lead to the accomplishment of our Mission Goals. Remember that your number one individual Crew Goal is one of the top five Mission Goals of Dylan IT. I will make time to meet with you all regularly from here on," Tom stated confidently.

"My only other comment," I said, "is to remind everyone of the need to focus on implementation. Implementation is rarely seamless. There will be obstacles, barriers, and challenges in implementing the Mission Plan. However, if you pull together and assist each other, implementation will be achieved."

The management team left Tom and me to finish our meeting.

With a little tweaking, Tom and I drafted the final version of the Mission Plan to be presented at the Crew Launch.

MISSION PLAN—DYLAN IT

Niche	Mission Goals	Management Team
Manufacturers & Distributors National—Australia.	**1. Business Performance**—Implement Mission Plan. Deliver Mission Goals. Meet Sales Revenue target of $3M at a Gross Profit of $1.08M (36%). (Tom/Jimmy) **2. Products & Services**—Review & develop products/services, pricing, and niche market. (Jimmy) **3. Crew**—Develop, document, and implement individual Crew Goals & manage IT Consulting Team. (Livy) **4. Systems**—Develop, document, and implement the systemization of Dylan IT business processes. (Willy) **5. Marketing & Sales**—Develop and implement a Marketing Plan and sales-based activities to communicate with niche to hit sales/gross profit targets. (Charlie)	**Tom** Managing Director **Jimmy Operations** Operations Manager **Livy Consulting** Senior Consultant **Willy Finance** Finance & Admin Manager **Charlie Sales** Sales Manager
Dylan IT specializes in IT products and services exclusive to the Australian Manufacturing & Distribution Sector.	**CREW GOALS** Every crew member, including Managers, have five (5) Crew Goals issued to them. Their performance and remuneration are appraised against these Crew Goals. Crew Goal achievement leads to the achievement of Mission Goals.	**STAKEHOLDERS** • Customers • Employees • Shareholders • Suppliers

MISSION PLAN—DYLAN IT (continued)

Mission Meetings	Mission Management	Dashboard Reporting
Weekly • Crew Operations Meeting • IT Operations Meeting • Sales Meeting • Finance & Business Admin Meeting **Monthly** • Management Team Meeting **Quarterly** • Quarterly Crew Meeting	**Crew Reviews** Manager meets 1-1 monthly with individual crew members to review progress on Crew Goals. **Annual Performance Reviews** Manager meets 1-1 with individual crew members annually to review performance, not remuneration **Annual Remuneration Reviews** Manager meets 1-1 with individual crew members annually to review performance and remuneration	**Monthly Reporting Pack:** Includes Profit & Loss, Balance Sheet, Aged Debtors, Aged Creditors, & Cashflow Report. (Willy) **Niche Metrics** (Jimmy/ Charlie) **IT Consulting Statistics** (Livy) **Sales Statistics** (Charlie) **Mission Meeting Register** (Willy)
Mission Meetings are scheduled at a standard recurring time with a fixed agenda. A Chair and Scribe are nominated for each meeting and rotated. Mission Meeting notes are circulated by Scribes by close of business on meeting day.	Managers attend Crew Reviews, Annual Performance Reviews, & Annual Remuneration Reviews. Tom attends ALL Annual Remuneration Reviews.	Managers support compilation of the individual dashboard reports. Willy issues dashboard reporting to the management team by Day 15 of the current month for the prior month's business performance.

Tom and I made some arrangements for our next meeting—the Crew Launch. This launch would be the single most important team meeting in Dylan IT's history.

I left Tom to book an external function room for the Crew Launch.

We were ready.

MISSION LOG

Niche Me Up, Scotty

- Tom explains to the management team each manager's individual role within the Mission Plan.

- Tom responds to fears and objections around the decision for Dylan IT to exclusively service the manufacturing and distribution sector.

- Tom introduces three software programs and three corresponding service-level agreements (SLAs) to the management team.

- Tom clarifies how customers outside the manufacturing and distribution sector will be managed.

- Tom demands the management team focus on implementation through this phase.

- Tom and I finalize the Mission Plan for the Crew Launch.

CHAPTER 13

Crew Launch

As the first of the managers joined Tom and me in the country club private room, the morning sun gently dried the light dew on the pristine lawn outside the window.

"Come in, Jimmy," Tom welcomed. "Take a seat."

Tom congratulated Jimmy on the formalization of his role as Operations Manager. He emphasized the need for Jimmy to impose himself on the team and improve the operational effectiveness and efficiency of Dylan IT. Tom reiterated his support that he would, as promised, make time to support Jimmy in his new role.

Tom revisited Jimmy's individual Crew Goals, which now included budget targets.

Jimmy—Operations Manager: Crew Goals

1. **Business Performance**—Implementation of Mission Plan. Deliver Mission Goals. Meet sales revenue target of $3 million at a gross profit of $1.08 million (36%) per Mission Plan.

2. **Products and Services**—Review and develop products/services, pricing, and niche market.

3. **Operational Management**—Accountability for the day-to-day operational running of Dylan IT. Responsibility for the management and overall performance of the management team—Livy, Charlie, and Willy.

4. **IT Consulting Team**—Drive, support, and manage Livy on the overall performance of the IT Consulting Team.

5. **Business Administration**—Accountability for ensuring all Crew Reviews and Mission Meetings are held with follow-up actions attended to. Responsibility for the business administration of Dylan IT. Complete MBA over next four years.

We then spoke of Livy Consulting and the need for Jimmy to manage and support her. Jimmy explained that he had met with Livy to discuss this and felt comfortable.

Tom had considered my suggestion to increase the managers' Total Remuneration Packages. In the case of Jimmy, Tom had generously decided to increase his TRP by $20,000. Tom felt that this was only fair, given Jimmy's increased responsibility.

Jimmy was very humble and flattered upon hearing of this pay increase.

"Is there anything you want to comment on, Jimmy?" Tom asked.

"Well," Jimmy said, "you might be curious to know that I got a job offer this week."

"What?" Tom exclaimed in a panicked tone.

"Don't panic, Tom. I'm not going anywhere. Peter Perfect rang me out of the blue. He asked me if I would consider moving to join him, and pressed me to bring Livy with me."

"What did you say to him?" Tom blurted.

"I told him no, of course. Peter's a slime-bag. I'd never work for him. I can't handle that whole game-show-host act he puts on."

"What about Livy? Have you told her?" Tom queried.

"Yeah, I did. She just laughed. Livy is too honest for Peter Perfect and too loyal to you to even consider it. Maybe don't mention it to Livy, Tom. She'll get all embarrassed."

"I appreciate your comments and the way you handled it. Thanks, Jimmy," Tom said. "Let's leave it at that."

"On that note, you'd better get Livy to come in and see us before the launch," Tom suggested.

Livy Consulting joined us shortly after, smiling as always.

Tom welcomed Livy and congratulated her on being the Senior Consultant for Dylan IT. No doubt it would be a busy role for her in managing seven IT consultants.

"How are you feeling about the role, Livy?" Tom asked.

"Really good, thanks, Tom," she said. "I've been doing a lot of operational management anyway with the exception of Crew Reviews, Annual Performance Reviews, and Annual Remuneration Reviews. The big challenge will be to drag up the chargeable hours from 50% to 75% and beyond. But that's a great challenge, and if I can't do that, we've probably got the wrong IT Consulting Team."

"The SLAs will help recover more of the IT consultants' time," Tom added.

"Agreed," said Livy, nodding.

"Jimmy tells me he has met with you to discuss the two of you working together with him as your direct report. Is that okay?" Tom asked.

"Yes. Jimmy has been fantastic in supporting me already. I have no doubt he will be a great manager to guide me."

Tom then shared the good news with Livy that her TRP was to be increased immediately by $10,000 in light of the formalization of her new role as Senior Consultant.

Livy was thrilled and a bit lost for words.

Tom revisited Livy's individual Crew Goals, which were:

Livy—Senior Consultant: Crew Goals

1. **Crew Goals**—Develop, document, and implement individual Crew Goals.

2. **IT Consulting Team**—Accountability for operational management of the IT Consulting Team. Ensure Mission Meetings for IT Consulting Team are held and follow-up actions completed.

3. **Financial Performance of IT Consulting Team**—Accountable for meeting or exceeding Revenue and Gross Profit targets for the IT Consulting Team.

4. **Crew Reviews**—Schedule and conduct Crew Reviews for IT Consulting Team.

5. **Professional and Personal Development**—Attend HR and management training course. Complete business degree.

Charlie Sales bounced into the room in his typical gregarious fashion. He was a colorful salesman, our Charlie.

Tom and Charlie had met up a number of times to work on the transition to the manufacturing and distribution niche, as well as the Marketing Plan.

"All good, Charlie?" Tom asked.

"Yes, Tom," Charlie said. "I'm happy with our discussions so far. I am a bit worried about dropping the ball on our meetings with customers and prospects, though. It's all well and good to transition some customers away from us, but we have to replace them with newbies—new manufacturers and distributors."

"You're right, Charlie. I'm aware of the need to move quickly on this as a priority. Keep on my case about this, will you?"

"Will do, boss," Charlie said affirmatively.

Tom revisited Charlie's individual Crew Goals, which were:

Charlie—Sales Manager: Crew Goals

1. **Marketing and Sales**—Develop and implement a Marketing Plan and sales-based activities to communicate with niche market and hit sales/gross profit targets.

2. **Niche**—Follow niche market definition, transition out non-niche customers, and create marketing content for multichannel communication.

3. **Customers**—Conduct customer stocktake with Tom. Implement customer care model to ensure all customers are contacted periodically at the frequency agreed under the A, B, C, D, and E customer-rating model.

4. **Sales-based Activity**—Schedule and conduct a minimum of five (5) meetings per week with niche customers and prospects (manufacturers and distributors).

5. **Education**—Complete marketing degree.

Tom shared the news of the increase in Charlie's TRP by $10,000. The handshake that followed nearly squeezed the life out of Tom.

Next in was Willy Finance.

"Hey, Willy," said Tom, ushering him in. "Darren and I understand you're a bit behind the eight ball in creating systems to support our very new strategy."

"Yes, Tom, I do feel that. The first thing I want to do is set up the software pricing and SLAs. I need to set up billing codes for both of those and help Livy ensure that the IT consultants record their time correctly against the job codes. Once we implement these immediate changes to the business, I can start on the systematization of business processes. There's some serious time in that, you know."

"I agree with your approach, Willy. Makes sense," Tom said supportively.

Tom then shared with Willy Finance his increased TRP of $10,000. Willy was delighted, albeit in his typical conservative manner.

Tom revisited Willy Finance's individual Crew Goals, which were:

Willy—Finance and Administration Manager: Crew Goals

1. **Systems**—Develop, document, and implement Dylan IT business processes.

2. **Dashboard Reporting**—Ensure monthly management reporting for prior month is completed by Day 15 of each month. Complete dashboard reporting on a timely and accurate basis.

3. **Mission Meetings**—Accountable for scheduling of weekly Finance and Business Admin Meetings ensuring follow-up actions are completed. Schedule and conduct monthly Crew Review with Ella.

4. **Finance and Administration**—Overall accountability for the finance and administration function of Dylan IT. Direct report of Ella.

5. **Compliance and Governance**—Ensure that all compliance and governance requirements of Dylan IT are met.

Tom and I then asked Willy Finance to request that Jimmy, Livy, and Charlie join us together in the meeting room.

With the management team assembled together, we issued the finalized version of the Mission Plan.

MISSION PLAN—DYLAN IT

Niche	Mission Goals	Management Team
Manufacturers & Distributors National—Australia.	**1. Business Performance**—Implement Mission Plan. Deliver Mission Goals. Meet Sales Revenue target of $3M at a Gross Profit of $1.08M (36%). (Tom/Jimmy) **2. Products & Services**—Review & develop products/services, pricing, and niche market. (Jimmy) **3. Crew**—Develop, document, and implement individual Crew Goals & manage IT Consulting Team. (Livy) **4. Systems**—Develop, document, and implement the systemization of Dylan IT business processes. (Willy) **5. Marketing & Sales**—Develop and implement a Marketing Plan and sales-based activities to communicate with niche to hit sales/gross profit targets. (Charlie)	**Tom** Managing Director **Jimmy Operations** Operations Manager **Livy Consulting** Senior Consultant **Willy Finance** Finance & Admin Manager **Charlie Sales** Sales Manager
Dylan IT specializes in IT products and services exclusive to the Australian Manufacturing & Distribution Sector.	**CREW GOALS** Every crew member, including Managers, have five (5) Crew Goals issued to them. Their performance and remuneration are appraised against these Crew Goals. Crew Goal achievement leads to the achievement of Mission Goals.	**STAKEHOLDERS** • Customers • Employees • Shareholders • Suppliers

MISSION PLAN—DYLAN IT (continued)

Mission Meetings	Mission Management	Dashboard Reporting
Weekly • Crew Operations Meeting • IT Operations Meeting • Sales Meeting • Finance & Business Admin Meeting **Monthly** • Management Team Meeting **Quarterly** • Quarterly Crew Meeting	**Crew Reviews** Manager meets 1-1 monthly with individual crew members to review progress on Crew Goals. **Annual Performance Reviews** Manager meets 1-1 with individual crew members annually to review performance, not remuneration **Annual Remuneration Reviews** Manager meets 1-1 with individual crew members annually to review performance and remuneration	**Monthly Reporting Pack**: includes Profit & Loss, Balance Sheet, Aged Debtors, Aged Creditors & Cashflow Report. (Willy) **Niche Metrics** (Jimmy/ Charlie) **IT Consulting Statistics** (Livy) **Sales Statistics** (Charlie) **Mission Meeting Register** (Willy)
Mission Meetings are scheduled at a standard recurring time with a fixed agenda. A Chair and Scribe are nominated for each meeting and rotated. Mission Meeting notes are circulated by Scribes by close of business on meeting day.	Managers attend Crew Reviews, Annual Performance Reviews, & Annual Remuneration Reviews. Tom attends ALL Annual Remuneration Reviews.	Managers support compilation of the individual dashboard reports. Willy issues dashboard reporting to the management team by Day 15 of the current month for the prior month's business performance.

Despite having not seen the Mission Plan formally, the management team members were well versed in its contents, and discussions quickly moved on to the Crew Launch.

Tom explained that while he had felt motivated to increase managers' TRPs immediately, he felt that increasing the crew's TRPs was premature and that it should be back-ended behind business improvement.

The management team agreed wholeheartedly. At 50% current productivity, a massive improvement from the IT consultants was needed. Willy Finance agreed that Ella, too, would have to step up in supporting him within the finance and admin area. It was agreed that a review of crew TRPs would be left until the end of the financial year. At the Crew Launch, this would be explained.

We then tabled the agenda for the Crew Launch, which was:

- Welcome attendees and provide background to the Crew Launch.
- Explain the Mission Plan with particular focus on Mission Goals.
- Introduce the management team and explain their roles.
- Provide a broad outline of Crew Goals. Explain that the delivery of individual Crew Goals by each team member will ultimately link to the delivery of the Mission Goals for the business. Explain that managers will schedule a monthly Crew Review with each team member, including the issuing of their Crew Goals.
- Provide a broad outline of Mission Meetings, Crew Reviews, Annual Performance Reviews, and Annual Remuneration Reviews.
- Conduct Q & A.

Over lunch the entire Dylan IT crew joined us for the Crew Launch. It went swimmingly well, with everyone embracing the changes to be implemented for Dylan IT and the Mission Goals for the financial year ahead.

When the IT consultants and Ella returned to the office, Tom, the management team, and I adjourned to the club bar for a few social drinks and informal discussion about the year ahead.

It was a great bonding session for Tom and his crew. Everyone was excited and buoyant about the future.

As I left the management team to themselves, I felt proud of Tom, Jimmy, Livy, Charlie, and Willy.

They were primed for success.

The Second Moon, Europa, would host them for a period of implementation. No doubt there would be many challenges to make the Mission Plan "stick," but I had faith in their collective abilities.

MISSION LOG

Crew Launch

- Tom issues Jimmy Operations with his individual Crew Goals and a $20,000 increase to his TRP. Tom is shocked to learn that Peter Perfect has approached Jimmy and Livy with job offers. Jimmy and Livy decline Peter's advances.

- Tom issues Livy Consulting, Charlie Sales, and Willy Finance with their individual Crew Goals and a $10,000 increase to their TRPs.

- Tom presents the final Mission Plan to the management team.

- The Crew Launch is held.

CHAPTER 14

Synergy in Space: The Right People Doing the Right Things

10, 9, 8, 7, 6, 5, 4, 3, 2, 1 . . . ?

We've all had that anticlimactic experience of listening to a countdown, only to see no blastoff.

In business, blastoff requires effective implementation. There is simply no point in devising, documenting, and launching a Mission Plan only for the parties accountable to fail to implement. Failing to implement is like a countdown without blastoff. All the hard work necessary to develop the goal counts for nothing if it doesn't get implemented. Everything prior to implementation is just fodder, wasted human endeavor.

I wanted to make sure that Tom and the management team didn't forget blastoff, so after spending a number of months on the Second Moon, it was time to check in on how the team was progressing in their new roles.

TOM

Tom really had led the way in conjunction with the management team. He had a large copy of the Mission Plan in his office, and regularly pulled out laminated copies in internal meetings so he could refer back to Mission Goals. He had a copy of every crew member's Crew Goals in a folder with him at all times. Tom had invested heavily in the management team and was working closely with them on all their projects. As the custodian of morale, he was personally mentoring each manager. The impact of this was that Jimmy Operations, Livy Consulting, Charlie Sales, and Willy Finance were highly engaged and felt deeply empowered. This flowed through the organization, and the morale and work ethic at the grassroots level had improved dramatically.

On a personal level, Tom had grown. He was a much more relaxed and happy individual than the one I'd first met. That big heart of his had opened up for all to see. He expected more, but also gave so much more. At work, the team saw a more human side, and they appreciated having more access to him through internal meetings. By letting go, Tom was able to encourage and empower crew members to learn and develop their skills. This delegation of responsibility created more time to focus on customers. Many of these customer relationships had been reinvigorated. Tom found he now had the time to review his products and services and focus on his market niche.

His private life had changed for the better also. Tom and his wife, Sarah, had "date night" set up each week. Tom had taken up memberships for the theatre, comedy club, and live music festivals. He'd even bought a share in a racehorse. His son, Jackson, was a budding young sportsman. Tom enjoyed practicing soccer and basketball with his son and attending his games. His daughter, Tyler, was a real girly-girl. She loved gymnastics and dancing. She was a real chatterbox and had such an imagination. Tom enjoyed taking the kids to cafés, the movies, and the park. He loved having time to talk with them, laugh, and watch them grow. He'd also reconnected with a number of friends that he hadn't seen for quite a while. Tom made a habit of meeting up with a friend each fortnight. As a result, those friendships had been rekindled. These changes had deeply touched Tom, and he shared this with me on numerous occasions in explaining he'd gotten his life back. "What a gift," he'd say, and he regularly affirmed that he'd never go back to his old ways.

JIMMY OPERATIONS

Jimmy was up for the challenge right from the start. He'd invested heavily in Livy, and the two of them were now driving the business operationally.

Jimmy had set up regular project meetings with Tom to work on the niche offering and their products and services. With Tom's and Charlie's input, Jimmy had finalized the three products, branded and sold to manufacturers and distributors as industry-specific products. In addition, the three service-level agreements (SLAs) were offered to niche customers. These SLAs had created regular annuity-based revenue streams for the business every quarter. In total, these six new revenue streams had added significant revenue and profitability to the business.

With Livy's assistance, Jimmy had established a weekly timesheet report that all IT consultants completed. He had tied this in to internal reporting with Willy, added it as an agenda item in weekly Crew Operations Meetings and the IT consultants' Crew Goals. After a slow start, Livy, Jimmy, and Willy had the IT Consulting Team complying with time recording. Even Tom filled out a timesheet. There were no exceptions.

The completion of timesheets had already raised customer billings by 20%, with time now being captured accurately and crew being more accountable for their productivity. Tom had already raised hourly charge-out rates by $10 per hour previously and had committed to another $10 per hour increase. In addition to these revenue accelerators, the impact of the three new software programs and three new SLAs would introduce new revenue streams. The overall impact of these revenue drivers would easily cover the loss of customers in the transition to serving a narrower niche of manufacturers and distributors exclusively.

Jimmy had been fantastic in assisting Tom roll out the Mission Plan. He single-handedly drafted the calendar, which drove mission management, and distributed it to all crew members. He went through it with each and every staff member, and even sat with them at their computers to ensure these meetings were scheduled in their online diaries. Jimmy was meticulous in setting the agenda for these meetings. He ensured that they were always held, started on time, and followed standing agendas, and that meeting notes were distributed by close of business. Tom had marveled at Jimmy's delivery on this. The leverage and freedom it delivered to Tom were significant.

WILLY FINANCE

Willy had diligently assisted the management team in establishing systems around the three software products and three SLAs. He had worked closely with Livy on improving chargeable hours and capturing IT consultants' recorded time.

Willy supported Jimmy to ensure there was an agenda for the monthly Management Team Meeting in order to confirm that the crew sessions were being held and that the outcomes were reported back to the management team.

Willy had implemented improvements to cash flow and reporting through meeting with Tom and Charlie in the weekly Finance and Business Admin Meeting.

CHARLIE SALES

Charlie had set up a number of project meetings with Tom to roll out the Marketing Plan.

Charlie had sourced a web developer and graphics house to create a new brochure and website. Tom had committed to writing a regular blog post for manufacturers and distributors. Tom was also in the process of writing half a dozen short articles for inclusion on the resources page of the website.

Charlie had spent significant time improving his understanding of the various social networking platforms. He also had a friend who was knowledgeable in Google AdWords and search engine optimization. These mediums would be dovetailed into the website functionality and features. Charlie and Tom had acknowledged how much work was involved in this. They agreed to create this content by the end of the niche-transition period.

For prospects, Charlie had agreed to attend the initial one-hour consultations. These leads would be identified from the various marketing activities.

For customers, Charlie set up a rolling calendar that would contact customers on a systematic basis. Based on the A, B, C, and D customer classifications, Charlie scheduled these, with Tom attending on a rotational basis.

Tom had set some initial revenue targets for Charlie that covered the niche-transition period. There would be higher revenue as a result of increased hours being billed, higher charge-out rates, and new products. However, this would be reduced by sacking D and E customers as well as advising customers in the future that Dylan IT will no longer service them should they not be manufacturers and distributors. Charlie felt the targets were still challenging because it was hard to accurately predict the net impact on sales revenue of those wins and losses.

Weekly Sales Meetings were being held as a core discipline.

It was agreed that Tom and Charlie would meet up with me closer to the conclusion of the niche-transition period and set new sales revenue targets once the new niche market offering was in place.

ON TO THE THIRD MOON

"I think we'd better book a flight to the Third Moon of Ganymede next time we catch up," I proposed to Tom.

"Fantastic," Tom said. "That's where I'll learn how to focus on maintaining my Mission Plan."

"Sure is, Tom. The Third Moon is where most business owners fall over. Some get complacent. Some get fat and lazy. They think that having devised a Mission Plan and implementing it, that's all they have to do. But they couldn't be more wrong. The secret is that Third Moon activities provide the coordinates to the Fourth Moon. The vast majority of entrepreneurs and business owners simply don't get this. Third Moon activities aren't sexy, shiny, or new. But I tell you what—they make you successful."

With that, I left Tom to reflect on his imminent trip to the Third Moon. He was ready, and I would be waiting to take him there.

MISSION LOG

Synergy in Space: The Right People Doing the Right Things

- I review Tom's and the management team's progress on implementing the Mission Plan.

- Tom learns that failing to implement is like a countdown without blastoff.

- Tom discovers it is time to leave the Second Moon of Europa.

- Tom is warned not to be lazy on the Third Moon, as Third Moon activities provide the coordinates to the Fourth Moon.

- The Third Moon of maintenance, Ganymede, awaits Tom and his crew.

THE THIRD MOON:
MAINTENANCE

Measure what is measurable,
and make measurable what is not.

—Galileo Galilei

CHAPTER 15

Predictable Space Travel:
The Rhythm of Forever Disciplines

Once I'd seen that Tom and his team had implemented the Mission Plan, I left them alone to manage their new roles. Tom had proudly watched this play out over several months.

I wasn't sure what Tom was expecting upon embarking on his initial journey to the Third Moon, Ganymede. I'd learned to keep an open mind. Different people had contrasting expectations and assumptions around the Third Moon. Third Moon activities, on the face of it, often seemed pretty boring. Entrepreneurs typically are great at working on new and dynamic content. It appeals to their sense of adventure and natural curiosity. Motivation levels are generally very strong on the First Moon, as business owners conceptualize, develop, and document their Mission Plan. Their work on the First Moon catapults them forward to the Second Moon where their desire for success and their intrinsic work ethic drive their strategy to implementation.

The challenge for Tom and the team upon arriving on the Third Moon was that they might experience a lull or a flat spot on their journey. They felt a great sense of pride and achievement in having created and implemented a strategy. That's understandable. Who wouldn't be proud of achieving that? But sometimes owners lose enthusiasm. The first two moons are but half the journey.

It's human nature to do something, then sit back and reflect on it. This is sometimes referred to as resting on your laurels. In business, the constant change and rapid pace do not allow owners to be dormant or static. The Mission Plan, once implemented, needs to be constantly maintained.

So I didn't know exactly what would happen when I invited Tom to enjoy a lunch meeting together on Ganymede—the Third Moon.

As soon as we sat down at our table, I began. "Let's imagine we're dining today at Gastro Ganymede. Maintenance is a big job, so it's fitting that Ganymede is the largest moon in the solar system.

"Imagine if you were to set up Dylan IT in space. You would need significant plant and infrastructure. You would have to have a space station for the crew as well as sophisticated life support and communication equipment.

"Getting it up into space is just the first challenge. How would you maintain it?" I asked Tom.

"I guess it would be like NASA's maintenance program. I understand they have a very detailed, rolling program to keep their equipment in space kept in perfect working order," Tom said.

"Yes, they do, Tom. In fact, there is much more regular maintenance work conducted than most people are aware. People are fixated on the big televised launches and media images. The media coverage of space travel is amazing. It's prime-time show business. However, the constant rolling maintenance program is very off-Broadway. It is invisible and doesn't get reported. No one is interested or really cares. But NASA does. NASA knows that if they don't attend to their maintenance program, launches go wrong, missions fail, and crew members die. Maintenance is actually the hard part. Relentless, constant, and demanding. It never stops."

"So we need to maintain Dylan IT like NASA maintains its space program," Tom added.

"Yes. You could say that, Tom."

"But it's all in place. The management team did all that on the Second Moon. You helped us to do it," Tom said, slightly irritated at any inference the Mission Plan wasn't now in place and being maintained.

He continued, "Everyone has worked so hard on this within the business. We don't need to question the management team about what they're doing. They've been so busy. I believe we have maintained the Mission Plan."

"No one is questioning their hard work, Tom," I said. "What I'm introducing is the essence of Third Moon activities—maintenance. And maintenance isn't sexy. In fact, Third Moon activities are about substance, not looks. Other entrepreneurs and business owners fall over at this hurdle. I don't want you and the team to. It's great that you're sensitive about being challenged on whether you're maintaining the Mission Plan. This passion and pride will provide the drive to honor maintenance forever. But first we need to seek the truth and discover any performance gaps. That's the first activity to attend to on the Third Moon."

I explained to Tom, over our main course at Gastro Ganymede, what he needed to do before we met up again for our next meeting. I spoke slowly and quietly, allowing him to take in these important instructions. My instructions were simple. Tom was to conduct a comprehensive review of Dylan IT's maintenance of the Mission Plan. He would meet every manager and assess each one's accountability. No one would be overlooked, including Tom himself. Following this review, we would meet together as a management team to discuss maintenance. After I explained this, we shook hands and departed.

At our next meeting, Tom assured me that he had followed up on my instructions. The management team joined us in the boardroom. I noticed Tom had his game face on right from the start.

"I thought it would be good to get you guys in today, with Darren and me," Tom said, "to conduct a review of how we're maintaining our disciplines and progressing on the Mission Plan. I must share with you that Darren and I met up last meeting off-site. At that meeting he proposed that I needed to be militant and methodical in attending to maintenance. Sure, we developed a strategy. We even implemented it. But how do we know that we're maintaining it? I was more than a little defensive about the inference that we may not be fully maintaining our Mission Plan and progressing on our Mission Goals. So as you know, I recently checked in with you all individually. I investigated the last three months, and I wanted to share with everyone the findings."

Tom pulled out the Mission Plan and started working through the Mission Goals set.

"This internal assessment of how we're maintaining our overall strategy and the strategies implemented is not a witch hunt. I want to remind everyone of our early sessions together where we pledged to play the issue, not the person. Well, I'm playing the issue today. All of our names, including mine, will come up in this review."

Tom went over the firm's progress on products, servicing, pricing, and niche market. Jimmy Operations had worked on this Mission Goal over the prior months with Tom's assistance. Three software programs had been branded and were now being sold to manufacturers and distributors. The three service-level agreements had also been created and released. The pricing on these six products had been finalized.

However, Tom had discovered that despite this progress, they'd failed to maintain the agreed timeline for Dylan IT's transition to its target niche market.

"Jimmy and I failed to maintain our commitment to the future niche market and the niche market transition timeline. I discovered, in catching up with Jimmy, that we had inadvertently taken on two new customers outside our specific target market of manufacturers and distributors. They were referral customers who went directly through to Livy and the IT Consulting Team. We agreed that we would not take on any new customers that weren't manufacturers and distributors. The flaw in our system was that we should've clarified more comprehensively with the team that all new customer inquiries must be directed through Charlie and me," Tom said.

"The second point relates to our agreed target market transition. We agreed that we would support all our existing customers that are not manufacturers and distributors for twelve months, as we transitioned into servicing the manufacturing and distribution sector exclusively. We were to call these customers and send letters to them confirming this. These phone calls and letters had not been planned as an action item, as we didn't clarify who was responsible for attending to this. So no one made the phone calls or sent the letters. Jimmy, please schedule a meeting with me off-line to list the customers that we'll call, and arrange for written correspondence to follow."

The management team noted down Tom's comments requesting that new customers be directed to Charlie and Tom, while Jimmy made a note to schedule a follow-up meeting with Tom.

Tom went on. "The next area I reviewed was the maintaining of Mission Management over the last three months. I caught up with Livy as our Internal Champion on this before clarifying the progress on the Crew Reviews with individual managers."

Tom covered the last three months in relation to Mission Management. Starting with the seven IT consultants, Tom had discovered that Livy had only completed Crew Reviews with six of the seven team members over the preceding three months. Jimmy had managed to complete his Crew Review with Livy, as had Willy with Ella. Tom himself had completed each of the three monthly Crew Reviews with Jimmy, but had completed only two of the three with Willy and only one of the three with Charlie.

"So let's close the loop on maintaining this, shall we?" Tom said. "Let's all report on our completed Crew Reviews at our monthly Management Team Meeting. But even more proactively, let's remind each other if it hasn't been completed before the month's out. Willy has set up these schedules in your diary, so let's use two-way accountability. I'm guilty of not maintaining Mission Management so far, so call me on it, too. Let's hold each other's feet to the fire on this. Let's commit right now to maintaining this without exception, okay?"

The team agreed and made notes to themselves.

"The next Mission Goal we implemented from our Mission Plan was Mission Meetings. Jimmy is the Internal Champion on this. Again, I reviewed the prior three months and our performance in maintaining the discipline of holding these internal meetings."

Tom circulated the table of Mission Meetings.

Mission Meeting Calendar

Mission Meeting	Attendees	Scheduling
Crew Operations Meeting	ALL	8 AM Tuesdays
IT Operations Meeting	Jimmy, Livy, and IT consultants	9 AM Tuesdays
Finance and Business Admin Meeting	Tom, Jimmy, and Willy	9 AM Wednesdays
Sales Meeting	Tom, Charlie, and Jimmy	10 AM Wednesdays
Management Team Meeting	Tom, Jimmy, Livy, Charlie, and Willy	3rd Wednesday monthly at 11 AM
Quarterly Crew Meeting	ALL	3rd Tuesday after quarter-end at 10 AM

Tom systematically detailed the meetings held in the preceding three months. One Crew Operations Meeting had been missed due to a public holiday. Two IT Operations Meetings had been missed due to Jimmy's and Livy's absence. Of the thirteen weekly Sales Meetings, Tom and Charlie had failed to meet on two of those occasions. Of the thirteen weekly Finance and Business Admin Meetings required, one of them was missed due to Tom deferring it without rescheduling.

Of the three monthly Management Team Meetings required, one of them had been cancelled.

Tom finally noted that the Quarterly Crew Meeting had been held.

"As you can see, there are many reasons and excuses for skipping the Mission Meetings," Tom said. "Holidays, key staff absences, deferral, and 'I'm too busy' are not valid reasons for not maintaining the integrity of our strategy. I know we've all been guilty here, but we're not going to succeed if we don't commit to this. I'm asking for zero tolerance on this. Again, each month at our Management Team Meeting, we'll review in detail that we've met for all our Mission Meetings on the calendar. If someone's away, we hold the meeting anyway. If the meeting date falls on a holiday, we reschedule. If we're busy, we still hold the meeting. Agreed?"

The entire management team nodded in unison.

"The next Mission Goal relates to systematizing Dylan IT's business processes. Willy is the Internal Champion on this one," Tom stated.

"I have scheduled a long meeting with Willy on this, as this goal is a project that will certainly take some time. So let's leave this aside for the moment. But rest assured Willy and I will be working on this. Willy needs to report on his progress within our Mission Meetings," said Tom.

"The final Mission Goal in our Strategic Plan that I reviewed was marketing and sales. Charlie is the Internal Champion here."

Tom admitted that he'd underestimated how much work there was to be done in creating the marketing collateral for the new niche. Tom had failed to write the niche articles that he'd promised for marketing purposes and inclusion as free resources on the website. The website was in mid-stage development, but needed more input from the management team.

"What if I helped write the articles and assisted with marketing content for you and Charlie?" Jimmy volunteered.

"Are you okay with that, Charlie?" Tom asked. "You'll still be the Internal Champion, but we sure do need some help."

"Yeah, that'd be great, Jimmy," Charlie said. "I must admit I'm feeling a bit stuck, between attending to sales and finding time for the marketing work."

Tom pointed out a positive, that the sales activities agreed upon were implemented and being maintained. Charlie had set up good processes around both new prospect meetings and the rolling systematic customer contact.

Then Tom looked at me. "So, Darren, you were right to challenge me about maintenance. I was defensive about this but shouldn't have been. This review of maintaining our Mission Plan will be a habit for life now. I understand why it's so important. We can all see the performance gaps and the tendency to slip out of the maintenance disciplines. If we allow each other to be defensive and put up walls when challenged, it creates a culture of 'near enough is good enough.' And we don't want that. Any one of us can challenge each other on maintaining our Mission Plan disciplines. If we don't, we won't deliver on our Mission Goals."

"It's these forever disciplines that set us free," I said.

"When we commit to the core," I continued, "we don't have to think about it. It's a 'forever discipline.' It just happens. Once we no longer have to allocate mental capacity to thinking about these disciplines, our capacity for core genius is increased. Our 'core genius' is the specific talent we possess that allows us to operate at optimal performance and make great things happen. I encourage you to spin the concept of maintenance around 180 degrees. Don't look at it as a boring chore. Rather, look at it as a core discipline that sets you free to embark on your most innovative, exciting, and important work. This is the gift of maintenance. It pulls you along on an invisible thread toward your goals—faster and more effectively."

The team acknowledged that this would set them free to attend to their most important work, and broke out into animated discussion about how they'd contribute to maintaining the business's core disciplines.

The meeting had been a great success. Not only was Tom onboard, but he'd also managed to convert the entire management team.

As the last of the management team left the boardroom, I turned to Tom.

"You did well today, Tom. You couldn't have done it better. It was great how you included yourself in not maintaining your Mission Plan. The team saw that self-criticism and humility. It was great leadership. Your use of specific examples to demonstrate the performance gaps in maintaining your strategy really helped to drive the point home. And finally, the invitation to call peer-to-peer on noncompliance, as well as reporting maintenance in monthly meetings, was a practical solution to compliance."

Tom smiled.

"Ganymede is rocky with light and dark shades," I continued. "Think of the light and dark shades as I suggested to you earlier on your journey. Businesses that fail to maintain, hide in the dark regions of Ganymede, hoping they won't get exposed for not maintaining their Mission Plan. However, we need to create disciplines around maintenance that ensure our crew occupies the light terrain of Ganymede. There, they will be visible, and maintenance will be transparent. Only business owners who thrive in the light of Ganymede get to travel on to the Fourth Moon."

I paused. "And one final thing, Tom."

"Yes?" said Tom.

"You will need Galileo's third attitude—perseverance. You, Tom, and the entire crew will need to carry perseverance with you during your time on Ganymede. The methodical and constant maintaining of your Mission Plan can be taxing. However, you now have structures within the business that should ensure disciplines are maintained. Just remember Galileo and his perseverance."

"I will, Darren. I promise to carry it with me indefinitely," Tom assured.

With that, Tom and I shook hands and confirmed our next meeting on the Third Moon. The next maintenance discussion on Ganymede would introduce the Stakeholder Quadrant.

MISSION LOG

Predictable Space Travel: The Rhythm of Forever Disciplines

- I impress on Tom that maintenance is the most challenging aspect to effective strategy. Missions fail without maintenance.

- Tom is defensive and agitated when asked to review Dylan IT's maintenance of the Mission Plan.

- Tom reviews progress on the five Mission Goals, with the management team noting where the Mission Plan has not been maintained over the previous three months.

- The management team commit to ensuring that maintenance is discussed and reviewed in future Mission Meetings.

- I explain to Tom and the management team that the maintaining of Mission Plan disciplines sets you free to focus on your most important work.

- Tom demonstrates great leadership through his humility and self-criticism in front of the management team.

- I call on Tom and his crew to occupy the light terrain on Ganymede, to be visible and transparent in maintaining the Mission Plan, and to not cheat or hide in the dark terrain. Only businesses that successfully occupy the light terrain of Ganymede may eventually travel on to the Fourth Moon.

- I remind Tom to carry Galileo's attitude of perseverance while on the Third Moon, as maintenance is relentless.

CHAPTER 16

The Stakeholder Quadrant: Customers, Employees, Shareholders, and Suppliers

om's arrival on the Third Moon had gotten off to a promising start. Tom and the management team now understood, acknowledged, and were accountable for the forever disciplines surrounding maintenance. I'd met with Tom to expand on maintenance in relation to what I called the Stakeholder Quadrant.

The Stakeholder Quadrant includes four groups:

1. **Customers**
2. **Employees**
3. **Shareholders**
4. **Suppliers**

Each of the stakeholders must be cleverly maintained on the Third Moon. They are different groups with different needs, each complementing the business in their own unique way. Business owners that reach the Fourth

Moon understand and respect the four stakeholders and are committed to optimizing their relationships with each of them.

CUSTOMERS

Customers want to deal business-to-business (B2B) with people that understand them. The global village has created greater expectations in what customers desire, expect, and require. They don't want the department store model. These niches and micro-niches are exploding, and B2B offerings must meet these emerging demands. The micro-niche phenomenon will only continue.

Tom had made a smart, strategic decision to service a specific market niche. Within months he would be serving the Australian manufacturing and distribution sector exclusively. He had formalized branded products to be sold exclusively to his niche. Tom was confident that a significant number of existing customers in the manufacturing and distribution sector would adopt and pay for these niche products.

Take Kevin for example. Kevin had been a customer of Dylan IT for more than five years. Kevin manufactured boutique metal wine racks for private clients. Kevin had been using the basic software Tom had developed for nearly five years now.

Following Charlie Sales's rolling customer visits, Tom had met with Kevin to understand Kevin's current view on Dylan IT as well as explain the recent changes to Dylan IT's business offering through branded software, SLAs, and servicing the manufacturing and distribution sector exclusively.

Kevin had been satisfied with the original software, although it had not been updated. In fairness, Kevin accepted that it hadn't been updated because he couldn't remember paying for it. Tom winced momentarily when reminded of his blunder at not previously charging for his software. Kevin commented that the service from Dylan IT tended to be ad hoc. Kevin made contact with Dylan IT only when something went wrong, and far too often responsiveness was tardy. Not to mention the billed amounts and delays in receiving invoices continually confused him. He'd never complained because he was loyal, having been a customer for a number of years.

After an extensive conversation covering the software enhancements and corresponding service-level agreements, Tom was able to satisfy Kevin that Dylan IT's new offerings would eliminate the headaches he had experienced.

It was a great meeting for Tom. He had listened to Kevin's frustrations, feedback, and current needs. Following the meeting, Kevin purchased the updated basic software program for $1,500 and took up an annual SLA for $6,000. Kevin also appreciated that Dylan IT was now specializing in his niche as a manufacturer.

But how would manufacturers and distributors that were not currently customers assess Dylan IT's niche offering? They would start with an overall assessment of the value proposition. Does Dylan IT have specific expert knowledge in their niche market? Do Tom and the team understand manufacturing and distribution pain points, frustrations, and goals? Do Dylan IT's products and services meet the niche market's needs through solving a problem or delivering an edge? These are just some of the entry-level questions a prospect asks, often subconsciously, in a few fleeting moments.

A prospective customer might next look at what return on investment, or ROI, they'll make in dealing with a new company. The ROI might be tangible, in seeking a return greater than the spend. For example, buying a Dylan IT product for $3,000 may generate $20,000 in extra revenue. Alternatively, buying a Dylan IT service-level agreement for $18,000 might save them $60,000 in salaries by not needing to employ someone. Conversely, the ROI calculation may be intangible. Choosing to enter a B2B relationship with Dylan IT may provide the customer peace of mind in not worrying about their current point-of-sale technology. ROI can be many things, but it's always judged by the customer. They choose. You don't.

Barbara ran a distribution business. Her love of fine china had led her to importing china from Europe. Barbara had a boutique business operating out of a warehouse with a small, motivated team.

Barbara had been a prospect, having contacted Tom following an introduction from another Dylan IT customer. Charlie had made an appointment to see Barbara as directed by Tom.

Meeting with Barbara, Charlie quickly gained an understanding of her frustrations and needs. Barbara and her team struggled with all the importation paperwork, transactional data, and inventory management. It was a huge headache. Customer relationship management was also a challenge in recording inquiries, order status updates, and customer histories. While Barbara's business didn't need point-of-sale capability, it did require an inventory module and customer relationship management. A couple of weeks after Charlie Sales submitted a proposal, Barbara purchased the intermediate software program for $3,000 and the corresponding annual SLA for $12,000.

Barbara was impressed that Dylan IT specialized in her niche. She liked the surety of fixed-price products and the quarterly fee for the SLA. Charlie had given her confidence that Dylan IT would eliminate many of the current frustrations she experienced within her business.

For customers to buy in to the Stakeholder Quadrant, they expect reliability and guaranteed supply. From day one they expect you to deliver on your promises. Deliver the hardware by Friday. Install the software and train us by the end of the month. Reliability also extends to returning phone calls and emails, attending meetings on time, and adequate preparation. It's about caring and delivering a consistent, predictable outcome.

For a customer to become a stakeholder in your business, it requires a relationship based on integrity and trust. You can't artificially manufacture an image of integrity and trust. It must be heartfelt, and be comprised of an infinite number of elements. It can't be faked or traded. It is a rare commodity that is exhaustively sought in business relationships. It is often best demonstrated in times of need, and our actions in these moments can create relationships that last a lifetime. And finally, customers do business with people, not businesses. Create winning relationships with customers based on these desires, and you'll create customer stakeholders for life.

EMPLOYEES

In our continuing series of meetings on the Third Moon, Tom and I turned to the second group in the Stakeholder Quadrant: employees.

To create winning stakeholder relationships with employees and maintain them, I believe you need to focus on six primary areas:

- Mission Plan
- Crew Goals
- Forums

- Performance

- Care

- Rewards

As I explained to Tom, over the years I've been asked by business owners to meet up with key team members individually. In these catch-ups, without the business owner present, the most common feedback from team members is that they have never previously worked for an owner who shared with them the company's Mission Goals and issued detailed Crew Goals to them individually. Employees thrive on this inclusion in understanding the vision for the business and the owner's specific expectations of them individually.

"Using Jimmy Operations as an example, Tom," I said, "he has blossomed from the moment you shared with him the Mission Plan and accompanying Mission Goals. He understands your vision and feels part of it.

"Targets interest employees. They want to know what the targets are for the business, and what their individual targets are. The business targets should be disclosed in the Mission Plan. Individual targets should be incorporated into the individual's Crew Goals.

"Jimmy Operations has clarity around the Mission Goals and financial targets Dylan IT needs to achieve. Jimmy's individual Crew Goals are clear and understood."

Forums are the lubricant for optimizing employee performance. On an informal level, this starts with the style and execution of daily operational communication between a manager and a crew member. At a formal level, these include the monthly Crew Reviews and the Annual Performance Reviews and Annual Remuneration Reviews held between managers and team members. These forums extend to the internal meetings contained in Mission Management.

Tom had given Jimmy freedom to set up many forums. He had direct access to Tom, a structured approach to managing Livy Consulting, and rolling operational contact with Charlie Sales and Willy Finance. Mission Management and Mission Meetings had been implemented successfully and were pivotal forums within Dylan IT.

"A good question to ask an individual is, 'What contribution did you make toward achieving our Mission Plan?'" Tom suggested.

"That's right, Tom. Jimmy, as Operations Manager, accepts account-ability for the Mission Plan. He understands how the achievement of his individual Crew Goals directly impacts on the achievement of Dylan IT's Mission Goals.

"For employees to become stakeholders, they have to believe that you care as an employer. Care is a bit like the integrity and trust sought by customers in deciding to be a stakeholder. But don't fake it. Employees rate fake care worse than no care. Create a caring culture in which you treat people with respect and dignity."

"Do you think I'm doing that, Darren?" Tom asked.

"Tom, you have demonstrated care toward Jimmy. There is nothing false about you. However, you have demonstrated this care more visibly through your recent behavior and actions."

Reward is the endgame for employees that deliver on their Crew Goals. They want their employer to acknowledge the time, effort, and skill they have contributed. They want acknowledgment and recognition for the results achieved, and ultimately they want reward. Rewarding individuals for delivering on their Crew Goals, hitting targets, or contributing to Mission Goals is pivotal to converting employees into stakeholders.

Jimmy had been delighted by his $20,000 increase to his Total Remuneration Package. He was even more excited to be asked to participate in an incentive scheme at the conclusion of the financial year. Tom's appointment of him as Operations Manager also was a reward for his contribution to the business and his loyalty. Jimmy felt rewarded.

SHAREHOLDERS

We moved on to discussing the third section of the Stakeholder Quadrant, the shareholders.

It would be easy to dismiss the notion of Tom and Sarah as stakeholders in Dylan IT. After all, Tom works operationally in the business, and Sarah is not operationally involved in Dylan IT. However, they both must adopt a stakeholder mentality.

"As you travel to the Fourth Moon, you must, as business owners, be able to separate your dual roles. Typically you will have an employee role, working operationally within the business. Beyond that, you are also shareholders of the business. The point I make is that these dual roles must be mutually exclusive."

Tom and Sarah must wear a different hat when analyzing the business as shareholders. They must ask the same questions, be objective, and adopt the profile of an external, passive shareholder in assessing their return from the business and its operational performance. This can be done. Sarah is the perfect foil to adopt the arm's-length approach required to fulfill the role of a Dylan IT shareholder. Tom, and his advisers, should encourage Sarah to request information and data to satisfy her questions and analysis while wearing a shareholder hat.

"But I can't do that!" Tom said.

"But you must, Tom. I don't accept the proposition that business owners can't assume a shareholder perspective because they fulfill an operational function within the business. They should be able to separate these roles and think independently under each hat."

I continued, "As shareholders, you and Sarah want a return on the capital you've invested. You must seek predictable, and hopefully increasing, returns from the business each year. Your lifestyle choices and financial security are ultimately funded by these returns."

"Go on," Tom stated. "I'm listening."

"You need to utilize a portion of these annual returns, beyond living and lifestyle expenditure, for wealth creation. Wealth creation in essence is the accumulation of investment assets over time, independent of current business earnings and salaries. These investments will create passive income for you and Sarah should you cease operating the business. Further, you and Sarah should seek to create wealth from any future sale of Dylan IT.

"Finally, Tom, as shareholders, you must proactively nurture winning relationships with the other three stakeholder groups. With customers, understand the lifetime customer value model and leverage this. With employees, seek to create job satisfaction, greater reward, increased retention, and optimized performance. With suppliers, seek to create long-term relationships around cost, service, and competitive edge."

Tom considered this, and said, "I guess it's hard to think of wearing the shareholder hat. For me, I'm too close as Managing Director. For Sarah, it's challenging because I think of her as my wife, not consciously as a shareholder."

"That's understandable. Wearing this shareholder hat when it's your own business can seem counterintuitive. Imagine if you and Sarah were third-party shareholders to a business. How would you think? What information would you seek, and how would you assess business performance? Different from the way you and Sarah view Dylan IT currently, I'm guessing."

"I've never thought of it like that," Tom said, reflecting on my comments.

"I'll speak with Sarah," Tom said, "and seek her support on wearing a shareholder hat when we discuss the business. It will help me step back from my operational role and provide an independent perspective."

"That's great, Tom. Remember to speak to her on this and encourage her to help provide a shareholder mindset."

SUPPLIERS

We then moved on to the fourth and final group within the Stakeholder Quadrant—suppliers.

It would be an easy oversight to overlook suppliers and merely view a stakeholder triangle of customers, employees, and shareholders that are all internal to the business. However, the insightful owner recognizes the contribution of key suppliers as the fourth stakeholder.

Successful owners value the role played by their suppliers. They see it as an inverse lens to the needs of customers as stakeholders. Tom wants absolute commitment from his suppliers. He wants a guaranteed supply of the latest hardware and software. He wants it at the best price and on the best terms. He wants a competitive edge through relationships, and he constantly looks for ways in which his suppliers can add value. Tom expects loyalty and is prepared to reward this with prompt payment, open communication, and reciprocal respect of suppliers and their staffs. And, just like his customer niche, he seeks regular communication and updates on innovative ideas and products.

"See how the supplier stakeholder relationship is simply the inverse of the customer stakeholder relationship?" I posed.

"I like the idea of a Stakeholder Quadrant," Tom said. "I'm going to introduce the concept at our next Management Team Meeting."

Tom wanted the management team to think more holistically about each stakeholder. In fact, it fit in perfectly with the Mission Plan and the individual Crew Goals of the management team.

He said, "Charlie Sales is accountable for customers, so he should be the custodian for customers within the Stakeholder Quadrant. Livy Consulting is accountable for the crew, so she would care for Dylan IT's employees as stakeholders. I will speak to Sarah about adopting a shareholder's perspective in assessing Dylan IT. I will encourage her to contact Jimmy Operations and Willy Finance if she needs to access shareholder information. And finally, Willy Finance is ideal to act as custodian for Dylan IT's suppliers."

"I think that's a fantastic idea, Tom. What a great discipline to bring stakeholder drivers alive in the business. That technique will be a winner for you."

"What's next on my itinerary while on the Third Moon?" Tom asked.

"I'm going to help you develop a spaceship dashboard for your reporting," I told him.

With that, I departed for the day, leaving Tom a bit bewildered. "A spaceship dashboard," he exclaimed as I walked out.

MISSION LOG

The Stakeholder Quadrant: Customers, Employees, Shareholders, and Suppliers

- Tom understands the role each party—customers, employees, shareholders, and suppliers—plays in the Stakeholder Quadrant.

- Tom's customers Kevin and Barbara respond to Dylan IT specializing in their niche.

- Winning stakeholder relationships with employees involves a focus on Mission Plan, Crew Goals, forums, performance, care, and reward. Tom reviews Jimmy Operations's experience in relating to these six areas.

- Tom understands that he and Sarah need to adopt a shareholder mindset in assessing the performance and investment return from Dylan IT.

- Tom reviews the important but often overlooked role that his suppliers play in the Stakeholder Quadrant.

- Tom decides to share the notion of the Stakeholder Quadrant with the management team, identifying specific managers as custodians for each stakeholder.

CHAPTER 17

The Spaceship Dashboard: Reporting on the Mission

I was sitting in Tom's office when he burst through the door carrying documents and muttering about paperwork.

"What's up, Tom?" I asked, seeing his frustration.

"I've been dreading this meeting, Darren. I don't even know what a spaceship dashboard is. This maintenance stuff, particularly in regard to reporting, has got me feeling a bit vulnerable again. This area has always been my Achilles' heel. Willy gets frustrated by my aversion to focusing on the business finances. My accountant is forever berating me about my taxes. Even Sarah and I have arguments over our personal finances. It's just not my thing."

"The first thing is not to worry," I said. "The past is the past. How would you feel if I told you your feelings are typical of the vast majority of business owners? Reporting and finance are one of the most common weaknesses in the hundreds of businesses I've dealt with."

"So I'm not alone?" Tom said.

"No, you're not, Tom. But the people who reach the Fourth Moon overcome this obstacle.

"Imagine, here on Ganymede, we're driving a lunar vehicle. Remember we want to occupy the light terrain of the Third Moon. Our maintenance work needs to be visible, and we need to see ahead while driving our lunar vehicle. The terrain can be rocky at times. Owners who overcome their weaknesses in this area, and reach the Fourth Moon, don't do it alone. They have other people in the vehicle with them. These people navigate and assist you with maps, resources, and charting tools. The people in the vehicle with you will include Willy, Livy, Charlie, Jimmy, myself, Sarah, your accountant, and other advisers."

"Must be a big lunar vehicle to fit us all in," Tom joked.

"Think of it as a lunar SUV. Plenty of room for all of us. I'm going to take you on a drive and we'll discover together how to set this framework up. Okay, Tom, put the lunar SUV into drive and release the handbrake. We're off.

"Willy Finance is going to oversee the Dylan IT reporting. Of course, he is going to source the reporting information from each manager, but he will be accountable for issuing it.

"To reach the Fourth Moon, Tom, you will constantly require regular and relevant management data. It is this data that will assist you in analyzing the company's performance and require you to periodically revisit the first three moons to review your strategy, implement changes, and maintain these changes before making your journey to the Fourth Moon."

I paused and then went on. "Think of the management data being reported and displayed on a giant spaceship dashboard. The dashboard has many screens, but you understand how to recognize the different screens and data. You and the team will learn to focus on the most important screens and analyze the data to allow yourself to lead, manage, and operate Dylan IT more optimally.

"How about you go and get Willy Finance to come sit in the front seat of the lunar SUV with you, Tom? He's going to be your right-hand man in navigating."

With that, Tom disappeared and returned promptly with Willy Finance.

We explained to Willy the need to set up a dashboard that would report management data on the business. While this data would be captured and recorded as frequently as daily in some cases, we agreed that we would use a monthly reporting timeframe. Willy committed to having the monthly dashboard reports available by the fifteenth day of the current month for the prior month's performance. For example, October reporting would be completed and issued to the management team by November 15.

"Okay," I said. "We are going to develop this entire dashboard in one session. Are you guys ready?"

"Yes, Commander," Willy joked.

"Tom's the commander here, Willy. I'm just the flight instructor!"

We established the monthly dashboard for Dylan IT.

MONTHLY DASHBOARD

Report	Manager	Mission Meetings for Discussion
1. Monthly Reporting Pack	Willy	Management Team Meeting
2. Niche Metrics	Jimmy/Charlie	Sales Meeting, Management Team Meeting, and Quarterly Crew Meeting
3. IT Consulting Statistics	Livy	Sales Meeting, Management Team Meeting, and Quarterly Crew Meeting
4. Sales Statistics	Charlie	Sales Meeting, Management Team Meeting, and Quarterly Crew Meeting
5. Mission Meeting Register	Jimmy	Management Team Meeting
6. Mission Management Register	Jimmy	Management Team Meeting

1. MONTHLY REPORTING PACK

Willy Finance is responsible for the compilation of the Monthly Reporting Pack, which includes the following monthly reports:

- Profit & Loss Report

- Balance Sheet
- Customer Receivables Report
- Supplier Payables Report
- Cash Flow Report

The Monthly Reporting Pack will be issued by Willy Finance to the management team by Day 15 and reviewed in the monthly Management Team Meeting.

Profit and Loss

I took Tom through a discussion of the profit paradigm. Many owners are fixated on talking about sales revenue. Sales revenue is important and it is a number we need to understand. However, profit is more important and I demonstrated this to Tom.

"If I asked you whether you want to own a transport company with sales revenue of $100 million, or a boutique manufacturer and distributor with sales revenue of $4 million, which would you prefer? Most people will jump in and emphatically request the transport company. But what if you discovered that the transport company makes a profit of just $400,000, or 4% of its sales revenue? On the other hand, the boutique manufacturer and distributor makes a profit of $1 million, or 25%, on its sales revenue. Despite the effort required in generating year in, year out sales revenue of $100 million, the transport company banks just $400,000 from its efforts. Nothing wrong with $400,000, but it equates to just 4% return on sales revenue. The little manufacturer and distributor has a niche market, and they do work hard to generate $4 million of sales revenue, but they bank $1 million. This equates to two and a half years of profit for the transport company."

"Yes," Tom nodded, "I'm aware of the fixation on revenue rather than profit. I often hear entrepreneurs boasting about the amount of revenue their businesses generate."

"Revenue for vanity. Profit for sanity," I replied.

Tom liked the sound of focusing on profit and what he could generate from his new niche market. He now had branded software programs to sell and had fixed-price service-level agreements. Hourly consulting rates had risen, and the consultants were capturing more recoverable hours through the improved timesheet system.

The Profit & Loss report would become a critical measurement tool within Dylan IT. In the Mission Plan, there was a target of $3 million of sales revenue at a gross profit of 36% for the current financial year. A Total Return (net operating profit plus Tom's salary) of $600,000 was the target against last year's result of just $300,000.

Balance Sheet

I then picked up Tom's Balance Sheet. From the Balance Sheet I taught Tom a useful little calculation I'd learned called "cash plus net receivables."

"Referring to the Balance Sheet, you add cash at bank to debtors receivable, then subtract creditors payable. In layman's terms that is 'money in the bank' plus 'money you're owed from customers' less 'money you owe to suppliers.' So if you took the cash in your bank account, received all the money you're owed today, and paid out all the money you owed today, this is how much money you'd be left with. It's an important number, as it tells you your short-term liquidity."

Tom had approximately $40,000 cash at bank and was owed $480,000 by his customers. Tom owed his suppliers $150,000. Therefore, Dylan IT's cash plus net receivables was $370,000 ($40,000 plus $480,000 minus $150,000). Tom needed to collect from his customers more quickly. He had nearly half a million dollars owing on a business that had sales turnover of $2.5 million.

"So if I got in all the money owed to us today and paid everything the business owed, I'd be left with $370,000."

"Yep. It's a lot of money, isn't it, Tom?"

"Sure is. I'd rather have it in my bank account," Tom said.

Customer Receivables Report

I then looked at the customer receivables report in detail. Customers on average owed money for sixty-six days. Dylan IT's terms were thirty days from invoice day. The poor historical compliance in IT consultants completing timely and accurate timesheets contributed to this. The invoices were leaving the office late, so it was no wonder customers owed the business money beyond their thirty-day terms. With the internal billing system so flawed, it compounded Willy and Ella's inability to collect debts.

Tom agreed sixty-six days for money being collected was too long.

Supplier Payables Report

Turning to the supplier payables report, we discovered that on average Tom paid suppliers in forty-five days. So subtracting the forty-five days Tom paid suppliers from the sixty-six days Tom took to get his money from customers, there was a twenty-one-day, or three-week, gap in collecting cash.

"So my customers are using Dylan IT as a bank," Tom said. "They have our money for sixty-six days and we pay our suppliers in forty-five days. They're getting free finance, aren't they, Darren?"

"They are, Tom. So let's focus on reining in those days outstanding."

Tom and I agreed to speak with Willy about cash-flow management, customer receivables, supplier payables, and reviewing our terms of trade. Tom noted to also speak with Jimmy, Livy, and Willy together about timesheets and invoicing.

Cash Flow Report

"Being on top of your cash flow is a critical Third Moon strategy," I suggested to Tom.

Willy would set up a daily cash-flow spreadsheet that plotted the predicted timing of cash inflows and outflows against the business's trading bank account balance. I also suggested to Tom that Willy introduce a rolling six-week cash-flow spreadsheet to project cash-flow movements in one document. Willy could present this in the weekly Finance and Business Admin Meeting, and discuss predicted timing of inflows and outflows. This would be a masterful tool as Tom, with Willy's assistance, would be able to conduct sensitivity analysis and see the impact of cash inflows from customers being delayed on the bank account balance. This would allow Tom to plan more effectively for contingencies before they occurred.

"The use of the rolling six-week cash-flow spreadsheet and the discipline of weekly reviews are pivotal to maintaining a healthy cash flow," I told Tom. "If cash flow is getting tight, you might decide to phone customers from whom you expect cash inflows in order to confirm the timing. Alternatively, if a likely shortfall in cash is detected, you might also decide to contact suppliers, explain the problem, and request to defer payment for a week or two.

"The investment in stakeholder relationships will foster the ability to contact customers and suppliers from time to time and ask for their assistance in maintaining cash flow. This is how stakeholder relationships synergize your path to the Fourth Moon," I said.

"I have another system to help you eliminate some of the stress around finance that you are currently experiencing. I call it the 'quarantine principle.'"

"You don't think I'm infectious, do you?" Tom joked.

"No, Tom. I'm talking about putting certain funds in quarantine, so they don't suffer the disappearing disease.

"Let's start with working capital," I suggested.

In simple terms, working capital is the amount of funds you have at your disposal to pay wages, suppliers, and other business expenses as they arise. I asked Tom what buffer of working capital, based on his risk profile, he'd be comfortable to have in the bank account at any time. Tom suggested that he'd feel more relaxed if he had one month's direct wages, indirect wages, supplier payments, and general overhead always available in the business bank account. Doing some rough calculations, that would equate to $60,000 for direct wages, $30,000 for indirect wages, $90,000 for suppliers, and $20,000 for general overhead expenses. In essence, $200,000 of working capital would cover one month ahead for all the business expenses as a buffer. Tom currently had only $40,000 in working capital, but he had $480,000 owed to him from customers. We agreed to build up the $40,000 in cash at the bank to $200,000 as the customer receivables were collected.

"So now that we have working capital covered, we'll turn our attention to quarantining taxes," I continued.

Tom and I agreed that wage-related taxes and other operational taxes would be cash-flowed by the $200,000 working capital buffer, as these amounts had been allowed for in this calculation. However, I suggested to Tom that it would also be prudent to quarantine funds for business taxes on current-year operating profit. Dylan IT operates in Australia, which has a corporate tax rate of 30%. I explained to Tom that if we established and maintained the working capital buffer of $200,000 in quarantined funds and then quarantined funds for the business tax payable of 30% of net operating profit, the leftover funds could be used to invest on the Fourth Moon.

"Will there be anything left after doing all this 'quarantining,' as you call it?" Tom asked.

"I promise there will be, Tom. And you'll sleep easy, knowing your cash flow and taxes are provided for."

2. NICHE METRICS

Tom, Willy, and I created a table of niche metrics. We wanted to record our customers' activity in total and then split it into niche customers (manufacturing and distribution sector) and non-niche customers (other sectors). In doing so, we could analyze this data on a monthly and year-to-date basis. The key driver would be to see these metrics transfer from non-niche to niche in number of customers, increased number of transactions, value of transactions, and increased average transaction value. The big metric would be niche sales revenue as a percentage of total sales revenue. This must increase to 100% as Dylan IT is ultimately transitioned to serving manufacturers and distributors exclusively.

Niche Metrics

Total Customers	Total number of customers Sales revenue ($) of total customer transactions (month/year-to-date) Number of total customer transactions Average transaction value (month/year-to-date)
Niche— Manufacturing and Distribution Sector	Total number of niche customers Sales revenue ($) of niche transactions (month/year-to-date) Number of niche transactions Average niche transaction value (month/year-to-date) Niche sales revenue % as % of total customer sales revenue
Non-niche —Other Sectors	Total number of non-niche customers Sales revenue ($) of non-niche transactions (month/year-to-date) Number of non-niche transactions Average non-niche transaction value (month/year-to-date) Non-niche sales revenue % as % of total customer sales revenue

I went over the impact of these metrics with Tom.

"If you have ten customers who make ten transactions with you each year at an average transaction value of $10, you generate sales revenue of $1,000. That's ten customers multiplied by ten transactions multiplied by a $10 average transaction value," I proposed.

"If you were to increase each of these metrics by just 10%, you would generate sales revenue of $1,331—a 33.1% increase in sales revenue. That's eleven customers multiplied by eleven transactions multiplied by an $11 average transaction value. This is the power of compounding each step of the transaction. Growing each multiple by just 10% actually delivers a 33% increase over the sum."

"Wow," said Tom. "That's the sort of math I want to learn."

We agreed that Jimmy Operations and Charlie Sales would support the compilation of niche metrics.

The niche metrics will be issued by Willy Finance to the management team by Day 15 and reviewed in the following week's Sales Meeting, monthly Management Team Meeting, and shared with the entire crew in the Quarterly Crew Meeting.

3. IT CONSULTING STATISTICS

The act of recording, measuring, and reporting the IT Consulting Statistics would have a significant impact on Dylan IT's operating performance.

Tom and the team had agreed to drive productivity of the IT consultants up from 50% to 75%. That is, to charge 75% of their available work hours (forty hours per week) to customers. In fact, to achieve this, Livy Consulting had suggested a target of 80% productivity. The most recent month had measured productivity at 76%, which was a record in Dylan IT's history.

Tom and Willy created a table for the IT Consulting Statistics.

IT Consulting Statistics

Total Consulting Hours (Statistics for Dylan IT)	80% Target	Total Chargeable Hours (TCH)—month/year-to-date Total Available Hours (TAH)—month/year-to-date Dylan IT Productivity % (TCH/TAH)
Individual IT Consultants (Statistics by individual IT Consultant)	80% Target	Total Chargeable Hours (TCH)—month/year-to-date Total Available Hours (TAH)—month/year-to-date Individual Productivity % (TCH/TAH)

Tom explained these metrics to Livy Consulting.

"Livy, we need your support in the compilation of IT Consulting Statistics."

"I'll make sure I get this input data to Willy on time," Livy replied.

IT Consulting Statistics will be issued to the management team by Willy Finance on Day 15. This will be reviewed in the monthly Management Team Meeting and shared with the entire crew in the Quarterly Crew Meeting.

Individual IT Consulting Statistics for each IT consultant will be reported to each crew member in Crew Reviews, Annual Performance Reviews, and Annual Remuneration Reviews.

4. SALES STATISTICS

Willy had recently met with Charlie and Tom to discuss and table some metrics around sales.

A Sales Statistics table was created.

Sales Statistics

Total Sales Revenue ($)—Dylan IT	Month/Year-to-date ($)

Sales Revenue split by source:
   Software Program Basic
   Software Program Intermediate
   Software Program Advanced
   SLA Basic
   SLA Intermediate
   SLA Advanced
   Other software
   Other hardware
   Consulting
   Sundry Revenue
	By source:
	Sales revenue (month/year-to-date)
	% of Total Sales Revenue (month/year-to-date)

Customers	Total number of customers Number of A, B, C, and D classification Sales revenue by A, B, C, and D classification Number of departed D and E customers
Customer meetings	Target for month versus actual meetings attended Names of customers met Charlie/Tom splits on number of meetings attended
Prospect meetings	Target for month versus actual meetings attended Names of prospects met
Sales pipeline	Prospect pipeline (current $ value of prospect pipeline) Won, Lost, and Pending status New customers (name, product/service purchased, and estimated $ value of transaction)

Charlie will support the compilation of Sales Statistics.

Sales Statistics will be issued to the management team by Willy Finance on Day 15 and reviewed in the following week's Sales Meeting, monthly Management Team Meeting, and Quarterly Crew Meeting.

5. MISSION MEETING REGISTER

A Mission Meeting Calendar had been created.

Mission Meeting Calendar

Mission Meeting	Attendees	Scheduling
Crew Operations Meeting	ALL	8 AM Tuesdays
IT Operations Meeting	Jimmy, Livy, and IT consultants	9 AM Tuesdays
Finance and Business Admin Meeting	Tom, Jimmy, and Willy	9 AM Wednesdays
Sales Meeting	Tom, Charlie, and Jimmy	10 AM Wednesdays
Management Team Meeting	Tom, Jimmy, Livy, Charlie, and Willy	3rd Wednesday monthly at 11 AM
Quarterly Crew Meeting	ALL	3rd Tuesday after quarter-end at 10 AM

While the management team was jointly responsible for ensuring Mission Meetings were conducted, Jimmy Operations was ultimately accountable for them being held.

Willy Finance would simply maintain a Mission Meeting Register to record whether Mission Meetings were held or not. Exceptions would be reported in the monthly Management Team Meeting, with a "please explain" required on non-adherence.

6. MISSION MANAGEMENT REGISTER

A Mission Management Calendar had been created.

Mission Management Calendar

Manager	Crew Reviews (monthly)	Annual Performance Reviews (mid-year)	Annual Remuneration Reviews (end-of-year)
Tom	Jimmy Charlie Willy	Jimmy Charlie Willy Livy	Jimmy Charlie Willy Livy IT Consultants (7) Flla
Jimmy	Livy	Livy	Livy IT Consultants (7)
Livy	IT Consultants (7)	IT Consultants (7)	IT Consultants (7)
Charlie	n/a	n/a	n/a
Willy	Ella	Ella	Ella

All members of the management team were involved in Mission Management. However, Tom, Jimmy, and Livy were principally involved.

Willy Finance would simply maintain a Mission Management Register to record whether Mission Management was followed. Exceptions would be reported in the monthly Management Team Meeting, with a "please explain" required on non-adherence.

———

Willy Finance had been sitting quietly, taking notes on the information he would need to display on the spaceship dashboard.

"Are you clear on this accountability for dashboard reporting, Willy?" I asked.

"I'm very clear on it, Darren. This reporting will provide the management team with analysis on the company's performance like we've never had before. We will be able to pull relevant data into Mission Meetings and Mission Management. Tom, the management team, and the crew will finally all have access to timely and accurate data," Willy replied.

"As long as you can consistently get the dashboard reporting issued by the fifteenth of each month, of course," I said.

"It's one of my individual Crew Goals, Darren. I have to be accountable for it," Willy quipped with a wink.

Willy Finance left the room carrying a bunch of notes he'd taken.

"I want to keep pushing hard on the Third Moon, Darren," Tom said. "We have momentum on this maintenance stuff. What's next?"

"We'll get Willy Finance back in again for our next meeting. One of our Mission Goals still to do on Ganymede is the systematization of business processes for Dylan IT. You and the team have already created some key systems, but Willy has to help you document and implement all of these systems comprehensively across the business."

It had been a heavy three-hour session. But much had been achieved. The spaceship dashboard had been developed and programmed.

Willy Finance just had to plug it in.

MISSION LOG

The Spaceship Dashboard: Reporting on the Mission

- Willy Finance joins Tom and me to develop dashboard reporting. The dashboard reports important data to the management team and crew. This data is measured, reported, and analyzed to optimize business performance.

- Willy Finance accepts accountability for dashboard reporting to be issued by Day 15 of each month on the prior month's performance.

- The Monthly Reporting Pack contains the Profit & Loss, Balance Sheet, Customer Receivables Report, Supplier Payables Report, and Cash Flow Report. Willy Finance compiles this.

- Jimmy Operations and Charlie Sales will compile niche metrics.

- Livy Consulting will compile IT Consulting Statistics.

- Charlie Sales will compile Sales Statistics.

- Willy Finance will maintain the Mission Meeting Register.

- Willy Finance will maintain the Mission Management Register.

- Tom and Willy Finance acknowledge the powerful impact that dashboard reporting will have on Dylan IT's business performance.

.

CHAPTER 18

The Universe Is Infinite: Establishing Systems

"Darren," Tom said as he sat down with Willy Finance and me at the head of the boardroom table, "tell us more about how you want us to work on our business systems. I'm curious."

"Systematizing business processes involves the drafting and documenting of key business systems," I said. "Each system is documented step-by-step to explain the business process, and is organized in chronological order. It's like a recipe for how we do things. A great pastry chef can produce the same high-quality cake time and time again by following a recipe that's been developed, documented, and perfected over many years. Once mastered, it's merely repeated.

"The recipe can then be passed on to other people, who—while perhaps less talented in the kitchen—can now produce a quality product true to the pastry chef's original recipe. You don't want the kitchen hand and apprentices making up the recipe and changing ingredients, quantities, or cooking times. The end product won't be high-quality or consistent, not to mention the cost of materials and time wasted. Customers will be upset by a poor product and by having to wait for the cake to be rebaked.

"Make sense, Willy?" I said.

"Sure does," Willy concurred.

"So we agree that the systematization of the business process will leverage business performance through delivering predictable results," I summed up. Tom and Willy nodded.

"Coming out of the kitchen and into Dylan IT, then," I continued, "we can translate this into not wanting crew members to make spontaneous or subjective decisions regarding our key business systems. We don't want our service standard to differ depending on who delivers it. We don't want reporting to be in a different format and distributed at a different time each month. We don't want the sales experience to vary between Tuesday and Wednesday. It's about consistency and quality in our actions and service delivery throughout the entire organization."

"But what about strategic decisions? They can't be systematized," Tom challenged.

"That's absolutely correct, Tom. Strategic decision making always has an element of subjectivity to it. The systematizing of business processes sets the rules for more generic decision making. This foundation creates capacity for your employees, your management team, and you to have clarity of mind when making strategic decisions. These strategic decisions are more difficult, and often the stakes are higher. After systematizing your business processes, you and your team will be better equipped to make clear, timely, and more informed strategic decisions for the betterment of all Dylan IT stakeholders."

Workshopping our approach to systematizing the Dylan IT business processes, we established a systems roadmap. It looked like this:

Systematization of Business Processes

Step	Action
1	Define current key systems.
2	Select participants for system creation.
3	Define how to create key systems.
4	Engage, educate, and train stakeholders in key business systems.
5	Update and maintain key business systems.

STEP 1 – DEFINE CURRENT KEY SYSTEMS.

After extensive debate, we settled on the following key business systems to form the nucleus of the systematization of business processes:

- Mission Meetings
- Mission Management
- Crew
- Products
- Services
- Customers
- Sales
- Marketing
- Suppliers
- Reporting
- Finance
- Administration procedures

We agreed that our niche market characteristics would need to be captured in these systems. Tom also encouraged Willy to utilize Ella in creating and drafting the business systems. The critical aspects of more than half of the key systems identified had already been conceptually developed on the First Moon and implemented on the Second Moon.

STEP 2 – SELECT PARTICIPANTS FOR SYSTEM CREATION.

We debated the participants that would support Willy in developing content for each key business system. We all agreed there was no point in compromising system content through limited input from key people, and we did not want to create any ill feeling by excluding key people from the process.

Having considered this balance, we decided on the following crew participants listed beside key systems:

- Mission Meetings (Jimmy & Willy)
- Mission Management (Jimmy & Livy)

- Crew (Livy & Jimmy)
- Products (Jimmy & Tom)
- Services (Jimmy, Livy, & Tom)
- Customers (Charlie & Tom)
- Sales (Charlie & Tom)
- Marketing (Charlie & Tom)
- Suppliers (Willy & Ella)
- Reporting (Willy & Tom)
- Finance (Willy & Ella)
- Administration procedures (Willy & Ella)

STEP 3 – DEFINE HOW TO CREATE KEY SYSTEMS.

I wanted to have some preliminary scoping discussions on how to approach the creation of system content. I'd seen many companies make costly mistakes in executing the systematization phase. Systems often took far too long to create, and ended up being as complicated as Tolstoy's *War and Peace*. Often systems were written in a language foreign to most stakeholders, resulting in them never being referred to or embraced.

I was also conscious of Willy's time and the time of other crew participants in contributing to system content. We had to find the right balance. If we delivered on the Mission Plan over the financial year, hit our targets, and won over our niche market, we'd be flying.

We agreed to write each business system in plain English using a non-technical, no-jargon style. We thought of Dylan IT's most junior staff member, Ella, so Willy agreed to write it with her in mind. Ella's comprehension and understanding of each system would be the litmus test.

We also agreed to aim for brevity. Each system would not exceed twelve pages in length.

We agreed upon a timeline. We would draft one system each month. The system would be reviewed, amended, finalized, and released in the month following. So after the first month, each month would include the drafting of a system and the finalization of the prior month's system. This would mean that the twelve key systems would be completed and issued over the coming thirteen months. As next month would be the final month of the existing financial year, Willy offered to commence with Mission Meetings and Mission Management immediately. The content had already been created and agreed upon, so these were the two systems' only required formal documentation. This would allow all systems to be completed by the end of next financial year.

The process of completing a system would look like this:

Timeline and Process for System Creation

TIMELINE	PROCESS
Week 1 (Month 1)	System workshop meeting attended by crew participants.
Week 2 (Month 1)	Participants create system documentation and present draft to Willy.
Week 3 (Month 1)	Willy presents draft of system at Management Team Meeting.
Week 4 (Month 1)	Detailed review and feedback. Participants and management present final feedback and amendments to Willy.
Week 3 (Month 2)	Amend, finalize, and issue. Willy amends and gets final sign-off from management team. Business system issued at Management Team Meeting.
Week 4 (Month 2)	Willy circulates hard and soft copies of system to Dylan IT crew.

This timeline would see the commencement of a new system each month and the finalization and issuing of a system by Willy Finance from the prior month.

We acknowledged that the systematization of business processes would put additional time pressures on management team members. However, Tom was the most affected, and he, in his new role, had additional capacity. The next most affected was Jimmy, who, with Livy having taken over operational management of the seven IT consultants, also had additional capacity. Charlie would be involved in three key systems being developed, which was no great burden.

The real hero here was Willy in taking on such a heavy load. Willy would be accountable for delivering twelve key business systems over the next twelve months. It was great to see him step up and add value in his role as Finance and Administration Manager.

The final element in system creation was format. We agreed to create all systems in Microsoft Word before converting to a finalized version in locked PDF format. Soft copies would be available on the company hard drive and all laptops. Hard copies would be issued in labeled color folders to all team members for easy reference within the operational environment.

STEP 4 — ENGAGE, EDUCATE, AND TRAIN STAKEHOLDERS IN KEY BUSINESS SYSTEMS.

Tom, Willy, and I next workshopped how we intended to engage, educate, and train stakeholders in the key business systems. We agreed on an informal approach that would be integrated into all our interactions.

For customers, our crew would incorporate system content indirectly into verbal and written communication. Charlie and Tom would complement this in their rolling scheduled site visits. Important aspects could be briefly mentioned and seeded at customer events on the social calendar. Finally, we agreed to introduce quarterly customer roundtable luncheons in the boardroom.

For crew it was simple. All crew members would receive the documented key business systems. Training would be dovetailed into ongoing Mission Meetings and Mission Management.

The shareholders, Tom and Sarah, would receive updates as systems were completed. System notes could be accessed by Sarah if required.

For suppliers, system content could again be incorporated into verbal and written correspondence. Further relevant content that suppliers needed to be aware of, or content requiring contribution from them, could be raised at inbound site visits or at key supplier meetings.

STEP 5 – UPDATE AND MAINTAIN KEY BUSINESS SYSTEMS.

"It is important to remember in the systematization of business processes that the universe is infinite. There is no horizon in space. Systems need to be updated periodically, and new systems emerge as businesses evolve," I said.

Willy offered to make any major changes required to system content immediately (we agreed this would be rare). Willy would conduct a quarterly review of one business system on a rolling basis.

New key business systems would be identified and nominated for inclusion in the firm's annual strategy session. It was agreed that a moratorium would be placed on the adoption of new key business systems until the initial key business systems identified had been documented and issued.

Having clarified the Dylan IT systems that Willy Finance would define and document, the meeting concluded.

––––––––––––

In the months that followed, Tom and his management team worked relentlessly in maintaining Third Moon disciplines.

Ganymede was a tough moon to reside on. Its sheer size meant moving around could be exhausting and sometimes monotonous. It was also easy to get drawn into the dark terrain where crew sometimes took refuge from their Third Moon disciplines. However, the dashboard reporting soon guided them back to the light.

At first, there was some resentment at being "called out" in not following Third Moon maintenance. However, once crew members realized that everyone would be held accountable, from young Ella right through to Tom, the crew began to accept it. Individual crew members started taking accountability through complying with the maintenance disciplines on an almost zero-tolerance basis.

Once the entire crew owned this culture of compliance, dashboard reporting was more enjoyable as the crew could focus on business improvement opportunities rather than on non-compliance.

Maintenance on Ganymede had stuck.

In our next meeting, Tom took me out to lunch at the Mitre Tavern Steakhouse for an end-of-financial-year celebration.

What happened that day at lunch showed me just how far Tom had come. Over a glass of Heathcote Shiraz, Tom made a personal pledge.

"As you know, Darren, it's been quite a cathartic journey for me so far," Tom started. "I remember that day in my office when I first met you. I was so out of control. I didn't want to hear your message right at that moment. I was frustrated and angry with my life and was toxic toward anyone who illuminated my state of affairs."

He sipped his wine and continued. "But I overcame that and we got started. On the First Moon, I was overwhelmed by having to create a strategy around my role, around the crew, and for the business. Looking back, I can honestly say that I was more worried about myself. I'd been hiding in my chaotic world and self-sabotaging the business. I can't believe how selfish I was. The impact on my team and family was terrible."

I smiled and let him go on.

"I initially thought you were imposing all this work on me—quite unfairly, I might add, with all those meetings and goals. But we developed a strategy for the first time ever. A real one, I mean. And I realized once we got going that it was working, so we moved on to the Second Moon.

"On the Second Moon we had to implement. That was personally and culturally challenging. The guys, me included," Tom said, pointing to himself in an animated manner, "were just battlers. We made stuff up as we went along. This strategy involved me working horrendous hours, expecting the same of the crew, and having little left for anyone or anything else. My business life created a vacuum in my personal life and nothing could get in.

"I remember asking you many times when we could leave the Second Moon and move on to the Third Moon. I was still impatient."

Tom took a moment to think, and then continued. "You used to tell me,

'Think of the patience Galileo must have possessed.' Well, I finally heard what you were saying.

"So I sucked it up and kept my head down, as did the crew, and we did do 'the doing,' as you call it.

"We got to move on to the Third Moon. Surely now we're on the home stretch, I thought to myself. And then you requested I do a review of how we were maintaining our disciplines and progressing on our Mission Goals. I couldn't believe it! As far as I was concerned, we'd developed a Mission Plan and implemented it. I thought the Third Moon was like going to confession—three Hail Marys and off to the races we go!

"I remember doing the maintenance review with the crew and discovering, to my surprise, all these performance gaps. It was very humbling. I learned from that discovery that maintenance never stops. It's like a circle. It never ends."

He could see I was eager to hear more, so he went on. "So a new financial year dawns. We're on the Third Moon, and I'm feeling great. I can't tell you how excited I am about the year ahead—on so many levels. But I need to ask you something."

Tom paused. I had a feeling what was coming. But I was wrong.

"Despite my prior form," Tom said, "I'm not going to ask you how long we'll be on the Third Moon. In fact, I'm not even going to ask if we've reached the Fourth Moon. If we deliver on our Mission Plan, meet stakeholder requirements, and I live daily as the person I aspire to be, the results should look after themselves.

"I trust in you implicitly, Darren. You tell me when we're on the Fourth Moon. Is that okay with you?"

Tom's heartfelt words and the honesty of his self-assessment were humbling. He understood the philosophy of letting go and allowing the universe to deliver. It was inspiring stuff.

"I acknowledge your pledge, Tom, in not constantly asking about leaving the Third Moon. But I do promise to tell you if you reach the Fourth Moon, though only when I feel you truly have.

"Deal?" I asked, putting out my hand.

"Deal," said Tom, and we shook hands.

MISSION LOG

The Universe Is Infinite: Establishing Systems

- Tom learns the importance of creating predictable results through the systematization of business processes.

- Tom and I identify twelve systems including Mission Meetings, Mission Management, Crew, Products, Services, Customers, Sales, Marketing, Suppliers, Reporting, Finance, and Administration procedures.

- Tom and I select participants to support Willy Finance in defining and documenting Dylan IT systems.

- Tom, Willy Finance, and I create a timeline and process for system creation.

- Tom, Willy Finance, and I workshop how to engage, educate, and train stakeholders in key business systems.

- Willy Finance commits to updating and maintaining key business systems on a periodic basis. A moratorium is placed on the introduction of new systems until the initial twelve business systems are documented and issued.

THE FOURTH MOON: LEVERAGE

The sun, with all those planets revolving around it and dependent on it, can still ripen a bunch of grapes as if it had nothing else in the universe to do.

—*Galileo Galilei*

CHAPTER 19

The Landing:
Tom's Arrival on the Fourth Moon

Twelve months had now passed since lunch with Tom that day at the Mitre Tavern Steakhouse, and he'd never uttered a word about progressing to the Fourth Moon. He was true to his word. Tom and the team had been very active on the Third Moon. What the team had achieved in just over two years since I'd met them was nothing short of amazing.

Since so few businesses ever reach the Fourth Moon, it's important to understand that it can take a long time to get there. There can be no absolute timeframes. From my experience, a start-up business that survives takes three to five years to really fire up. There are exceptions, but this three- to five-year rule has stood the test of time. For existing businesses like Tom's, it can be quicker or slower. On the one hand, it may be quicker for businesses where the infrastructure, niche market, and crew are already established. On the other hand, if the target market needs to be reeducated, the business doesn't have a premium offering, or the right crew isn't in place, these barriers can take longer to overcome.

The financial year had just ended. It was the second full financial year that Tom and I had been working together. It is always with great anticipation that I review a full financial year of the company's performance post-implementation. While the strategy had been devised and implemented during the first financial year, the business strategies had been in place only for the entire second financial year.

Callisto is a copper metallic color when viewed in certain light, representing wealth. Callisto's ancient crust has survived for billions of years. This lightly populated planet has plenty of room for the lucky ones that reach it.

And lucky they are, for they experience leverage. Leverage is a life-changing experience: a personal nirvana that Callisto's visitors never tire of, nor take for granted.

Leverage is about control, confidence, and freedom. The control to truly navigate your destiny using proven, time-tested success strategies. The confidence to know that your strategies work and are available to you indefinitely. The freedom to live the life you want and attend to activities you choose.

Leverage is about earning more and working less. The wealth on Callisto is limitless. The Fourth Moon's atmosphere is constantly replenished. This replenishment allows visitors to refresh and reinvent themselves. Few people experience stress on Callisto.

Leverage is a little like knowing next week's lottery numbers. Fourth Moon visitors know their success formula, and relax in the comfort of knowing they can revisit the first three moons to conduct mission work or repairs should they need to. That is the true wealth that lies within Callisto's ancient crust.

"According to Churchill," I said, "'however beautiful the strategy, you should occasionally look at the results.'"

Tom and I reviewed the operating performance of the two financial years since commencing our journey together. We decided to assess strategy from the perspective of each of the stakeholders.

The Fourth Moon of Callisto was within Tom's reach. He just didn't know it yet.

CUSTOMER STAKEHOLDERS

One of the biggest results of the year was the transition into the market niche of servicing manufacturers and distributors.

The transition into Dylan IT's new market niche had been an overwhelming success. Firstly, existing manufacturing and distribution customers embraced the change and saw the benefits that Dylan IT would bring to them by operating exclusively in their sector. This was supported by strong take-up of the new software programs and service-level agreements. Approximately 80% of the existing manufacturers and distributors took up a new software program and accompanying service-level agreement. Secondly, new customers from the manufacturing and distribution sector came onboard with the business. The niche market specialization was a big driver in Charlie and Tom winning new business. Thirdly, previously existing customers that were not manufacturers and distributors were generally accepting of the shift in niche. Some complained, and Tom handled these customers honestly and personally met with them. He introduced them to a handpicked shortlist of IT providers that they could turn to.

The only exception to the niche market rule was Bob, Tom's oldest and dearest customer. Bob had been a good friend of Tom's father. Tom promised to look after Bob personally. It was a small price to pay for loyalty and friendship, and it would not affect the crew internally or Tom's capacity significantly.

The business had successfully executed its customer communication mantra of "helping, not selling." Customer relationships had deepened through regular communication and contact. Customers felt they belonged. They enjoyed having industry-specific products and services that met their unique needs, and they were prepared to pay a premium for them.

EMPLOYEE STAKEHOLDERS

Jimmy Operations had simply done a wonderful job. He'd had a big year. Operationally, he'd taken on the role of Operations Manager with gusto. He allowed Livy Consulting enough rope to autonomously manage the seven IT consultants while still being involved and accountable. He developed strong cross-reporting alliances with Charlie and Willy Finance. He championed the design, rollout, and pricing of products and services into Dylan IT's new market niche with Tom. He also championed Mission Management, which now operated like Swiss clockwork. More importantly, he'd become a true second-in-charge to Tom. Tom trusted Jimmy implicitly. Many customers now contacted Jimmy directly.

While Tom might have been the commander on the mission, Jimmy was the pilot.

Willy Finance, too, had delivered for the year. Operationally, Willy had provided Tom with consistent support in finance, cash flow, and management reporting. He developed Ella's skill sets through delegation and on-the-job training. At a strategic level, Willy had overseen dashboard reporting and ensured that the management team and crew received and reviewed it faithfully. Mission Management had been a huge hit with all the team members. The output, job satisfaction, culture, and morale were off the scale. Willy had also drafted, documented, and issued the key business systems nominated a year earlier. He pushed through many barriers to get this done with these systems now alive throughout the organization and referred to daily. All stakeholders had embraced them.

Charlie Sales had a challenging year. He had to develop the Marketing Plan and sales activities to attract the new niche target market. At the same time, he had to migrate non-niche customers out of the business. He managed to pull this off. The other challenge was to facilitate Tom's creation of niche content for the website and marketing collateral. He had to push and cajole Tom at times, but he got Tom to deliver. Charlie then worked tirelessly outside of his sales calls with the web developer and Internet consultant to establish an online presence for Dylan IT. Despite all this activity, Charlie's biggest triumph was growing Dylan IT's sales revenue significantly, notwithstanding the dropping of D and E customers and narrowing of the firm's target market.

Livy Consulting had blossomed over the year. She was a natural at managing the IT consultants, despite the busy workload of seven direct reports plus her own consulting work. She was firm but fair, with a caring attitude. Livy knew when to hit and when to hug. She could read people, especially IT people. The crew adored her and respected her unequivocally. She built a strong relationship with Jimmy as her manager, worked across sales and customer care with Charlie and Tom, and assisted Willy and Ella with the back-end office administration. With the most crew to manage, she was also the biggest contributor to the success of Mission Meetings and Mission Management. Beyond her management contribution, Livy's big win for the year was achieving a 100% timesheet compliance record (timesheets completed accurately and on time) and dragging chargeable hours for the IT Consulting Team up from 50% to 85%.

SHAREHOLDER STAKEHOLDERS

We reviewed the success of our strategy in relation to shareholder stakeholders.

The results were in. The financial year had been a huge success. Here are the profits and losses, comparing the two years post-implementation (Years 2 and 3), with Tom's profits and losses of three years ago, before meeting him (Year 1).

	Year 1 Actual (3 years prior)	Year 2 Actual Last Year	Year 2 Budget Last Year	Year 3 Actual This Year	Year 3 Budget This Year
Sales Revenue	$2,500,000	$2,820,000	$3,000,000	$4,000,000	$3,200,000
Direct Costs (IT consulting wages and software/ hardware materials)	$1,750,000	$1,861,000	$1,920,000	$2,480,000	$2,048,000
Gross Profit	$750,000 (30%)	$959,000 (34%)	$1,080,000 (36%)	$1,520,000 (38%)	$1,152,000 (36%)
Indirect Wages	$375,000	$420,000	$420,000	$500,000	$490,000
General Overhead expenses	$200,000	$201,000	$210,000	$220,000	$212,000
Operating Profit	$175,000 (7%)	$338,000 (12%)	$450,000 (15%)	$800,000 (20%)	$450,000 (14%)
Add Tom's salary back	$125,000	$155,000	$150,000	$200,000	$200,000
Total Return	$300,000	$493,000	$600,000	$1,000,000	$650,000

What a result! Sales revenue had grown by 60% from $2.5 million to $4.0 million. Gross profit had increased from 30% to 38%. Operating profit had increased from $175,000 (7%) to $800,000 (20%). So Tom and Sarah's shareholder return of $800,000, when added to Tom's operational salary of $200,000 (he'd increased this from his original $125,000), meant Tom and Sarah were now pulling $1 million from the business—an amazing achievement.

"We sure have been lucky," Tom said.

"Hey, these results are no fluke," I told him.

Ignore the intangibles in strategy for a moment, and let's look at the profit drivers. It is the composite effect of all these factors that allowed Tom's Total Return to explode. These included:

- Higher hourly charge-out rates (increased by $20 per hour; $10 in Year 1 and $10 in Year 2)
- More billable hours (up to 85% from 50%)
- Three new software programs introduced (three new product-revenue streams)
- Three new products introduced through SLAs (three new SLA revenue streams)
- Higher profit margins on new products introduced
- Higher profit margins on new services introduced

"These results weren't luck, Tom," I told him. "Dylan IT made them happen."

SUPPLIER STAKEHOLDERS

Supplier relationships had blossomed over the year. Willy and Ella had negotiated better credit terms with regular and volume suppliers. Niche market suppliers started making more site visits once they understood the change in Dylan IT's target market. Two suppliers offered exclusivity on certain components, while another supplier provided in-house training for the IT Consulting Team. Overall, supplier relationships were stronger than ever.

In summary, Churchill's results were in. It wasn't just a beautiful strategy, but also beautiful results.

"How much has your life changed since I met you just over two years ago?" I asked Tom.

"Well, I hope I'm a little different now compared to the Busy Fool you met that first day," Tom joked.

"We've all been the Busy Fool at some stage, Tom, often in our formative years. It is a matter of identifying that and escaping it."

"To get back to your question," Tom said, "life has changed a lot. I took a six-week holiday last year, which is more than I've taken in the previous five years. With the help of the crew, I'm able to work fewer hours during the week. I don't work evenings anymore and never work weekends—though I used to do that a lot. I've probably gone from sixty-five hours a week to forty-five hours or less. This new financial year I'm shifting to more four-day weeks, and I'm taking mid-year and end-of-year holiday breaks. You're right about how less is more.

"On the personal side, life continues to thrive. Sarah and I haven't been happier in years. We have kept up date night and enjoy our music and theatre. Sarah says I'm more relaxed, and that I remind her of the guy she married. Having time available for Jackson and Tyler is amazing. We look forward to our weekends together, and the kids choose holiday activities that we plan for. I've reconnected with my dear old parents. We visit them with Sarah and the kids on alternate fortnights. They come to all the kids' activities as well. And I'm finally making time to invest in my friends, which has been a real buzz. We catch up for tennis each week and watch that slow racehorse go around. Some business friends and I have gotten involved in a charity supporting disadvantaged youth. That's been particularly rewarding."

"Well, Tom, I think you just gave me the best description of leverage I've ever heard. You're working less, and earning more money. You enjoy activities of choice. You're connecting in amazing ways with your family, friends, and community. Your stakeholders are all satisfied. You've leveraged your life." I smiled at Tom's success.

"And there's one more thing I need to tell you, Tom." I spoke in a serious and somber tone. "It is with deep consideration and reflection that I share this with you. It's something very important and personal to you. Can I share it with you now?"

"Yes, what is it?" Tom asked, looking momentarily concerned.

"You've reached the Fourth Moon. Welcome to Callisto!" I shouted.

Tom's face lit up like a NASA space launch.

"Really?" he said. "I know I promised never to ask last year at lunch, but that's fantastic. I promised myself to put it in the back of my mind. Still, it's unbelievable."

"You deserve it, mate. Marketing guru Seth Godin calls it 'the dip'—the dip is the hard bit on the journey where most people give up. It's like a twenty-mile marker in a marathon. You dug in and kept going. That's what it takes to reach the Fourth Moon. How does it feel?"

"It feels exhilarating. I'm pumped." Tom paused. I could see he was pleased. "It's been great to review the past two years together here today. I can see in everything we've covered that I really have arrived on the Fourth Moon. I appreciate all your help so far." His eyes were glazed with the emotion of his achievement.

"Now that we're on Callisto, let's have some fun. There's so much to explore on this moon, and it's all good. We'll meet up in a couple of weeks and get into it. In the meantime, let me shout you a beer to celebrate reaching the Fourth Moon."

Tom and I went to the Rising Sun Hotel to celebrate. The night kicked on, and perhaps a bit too much merriment was had. For Tom, it was recognition and celebration of nearly two years of hard work. For me, the dedication to help Tom and the crew succeed on their mission felt vindicating. He told me he'd remember this night forever. The cynic in me said it was the drink talking. The dreamer in me told me he would. I believe the dreamer was right.

(Note: The Mission Logs appearing at the end of each chapter within the first three moons summarize Tom's lessons and actions on his journey. These Mission Logs are no longer required in this final section of the book, as Tom has successfully reached the Fourth Moon.)

CHAPTER 20

Tom's Payday:
Sharing the Spoils of Victory,
Writing the Checks, and the Power
of Multiple Income Streams

T om was truly energized in reaching the Fourth Moon, and was looking forward to talking about money and rewards after we recovered
from our celebration. But we needed to do a quick review of how
Tom had done over the most recent financial year in managing cash flow
and quarantining funds.

"Remember back on the Third Moon when we set up the cash-flow
reserves for working capital and business tax?" I recalled to Tom.

"Yes," Tom said. "I wanted $200,000 set aside to cover wages, suppliers,
and overhead expenses for one month. We would then set aside 30% of
operating profit to cover the business taxation on earnings. Is that right as
you remember it?"

"Spot on, Tom, with one exception. Earning $800,000 in operating profit, you might need to set aside a bit more as a tax provision. Perhaps 40% of profit rather than 30%."

"Okay. Let's have a look at my reserves. We have paid all of the tax owing on Year 2, so it is just last year—Year 3—that we have tax payable on. I've also got Willy to maintain the working capital account of $200,000. The tax reserve is in an interest-bearing account and sits at around $240,000, which represents 30% of the $800,000 operating profit for Year 3. You'll be pleased to know, Darren, that I've squirreled away some surplus funds into a separate savings account. That account has a balance of $330,000. Of course, I've still got my debtors, which sit at $500,000; but even on the higher turnover of $4 million, these have been reined in to forty-five days outstanding."

"Good job," I said. "You were listening. As Matt Damon said in the film *Good Will Hunting*, 'How do you like them apples?'"

"Them are good apples," Tom said, laughing.

"So notwithstanding your accountant's ability to reduce your taxable income, let's work on your cash position and quarantining accounts using operating profit of $800,000 for financial Year 3."

Tom had his $200,000 working capital balance maintained each month, so working capital was fully covered. Based on the business profit of $800,000, we agreed to quarantine 40% of business tax on this level of higher earnings. This would require quarantining $320,000 (40% of $800,000) rather than the $240,000 previously estimated, resulting in an $80,000 shortfall for the business-tax provision. But utilizing the $330,000 surplus funds on hand in the separate bank account, Tom could transfer $80,000 of this to the business-tax provision account to cover the shortfall, and the entire year's profit would be covered. This would still leave $250,000 ($330,000 less $80,000 extra business tax required) of surplus funds available.

I raised with Tom the opportunity to use the excess funds of $250,000 for personal use or as a deposit for an investment. Tom and Sarah had recently paid off their family home and Tom explained that they wished to set up an education fund for Jackson and Tyler. Of that surplus, $50,000 would be perfect for this.

"So we've got the business cash flows sorted, tax sorted, and home mortgage gone, and we've established a $50,000 education fund for Jackson and

Tyler. There's still, of course, the remaining $200,000 in savings you squirreled away in that separate bank account."

"Sounds good, Darren," Tom acknowledged.

SHARING THE SPOILS OF VICTORY

Before I congratulated Tom further on Dylan IT's incredible turnaround in profitability, I felt it appropriate to pull back for a moment and recognize the contribution the crew had made to the result.

"I know you're hosting a special dinner to celebrate and recognize what the team achieved this year," I acknowledged of Tom, "but I think it's also important to share the spoils of victory in other tangible ways.

"You've committed to Mission Management. And the managers, as well as the wider crew, received market increases in salary for their operational roles. I'd recommend that any further salary increases to key people and high performers be on the generous side this year, in light of their contribution and achievements. Jimmy, Willy, Charlie, and Livy have all delivered and are now operating at a management level superior to where they were when I met them. There is room to move here, Tom. It will be more than adequately funded by annual price increases and organic growth."

"I agree," Tom said without hesitation. "Good point. We'll do that."

With salaries covered, I now wanted to introduce performance-based rewards. There were three I wanted to seed with Tom. They were:

- Incentive schemes for management team members
- Incentive schemes for other crew
- Random acts of kindness

I proposed to Tom that the establishment of an incentive scheme for the management team would be worth considering. At this early stage of generating higher profits, it was premature to discuss equity with any of the managers, and there were pitfalls to introducing minority shareholders. I'd developed incentive schemes for clients in the past. They were based on quarterly and annual performance measured against predetermined budget targets. The benefits of these were many. Management felt more engaged and rewarded in receiving additional "at risk" earnings should the business achieve its targets.

It created a culture of win-win or lose-lose between owners and management, which developed an egalitarian mindset. It often resulted in a quasi-shareholder mentality within management whereby they'd think more like owners on expenditure, hiring crew, or writing off customer debts. It also helped with crew retention, as participants in annual incentive schemes had to be employed by the business at the end of a financial year to be rewarded.

Incentive schemes for general crew were a bit trickier. I personally didn't like points-based systems, as they often created cultural divisions or distracted crew members from the bigger game. My preference was to establish a discretionary pool from which the shareholders could distribute annually. They may choose to distribute all or none of the annual pool. I suggested to Tom that such a pool could be established for the new financial year ahead, and that employees still with the business at the end of the next financial year, having served the full year, would be eligible to participate in the pool. These discretionary incentives could be awarded in differing sums to none— or to many employees from the pool. For example, a $20,000 pool might be distributed between four employees for their contributions over the financial year, or it might be split among ten. These discretionary bonuses are, of course, quite separate from the Annual Remuneration Reviews I had discussed with Tom earlier.

The other rewards concept I'd seen was what I called "random acts of kindness." These random acts aim to create spontaneous recognition of exemplary work—for instance, if someone's gone the extra mile for another person (internal or external to the business), or perhaps as a way to celebrate a personal achievement or milestone. These random acts of kindness are best done on a non-monetary basis. They're more personal. The introduction of a new customer by a crew member might be rewarded with a holiday trip away. A crew member working on the weekend to fix a major customer's computer bug might get a long weekend off with pay. A crew member getting married or welcoming a baby might enjoy a special gift from the company. As long as the random acts are done spontaneously and from the heart, individuals will feel touched by the sentiment.

Tom had listened intently as I described these three mechanisms for sharing the spoils of victory with the team.

"We'll do all three," Tom said generously. "It just seems like the right thing to do. I couldn't have achieved the results we achieved last year without them. I would never have reached the Fourth Moon without crew members' help. We can afford it, can't we?"

"We can, Tom," I said. "Let's pitch it to them as a trial for the new financial year. If it works well, we'll keep it going. If it fails for some reason, we can review it. There is a maturity test required for these platforms to work. It's really up to them how they respond to it."

We agreed to establish the criteria of these three schemes together, update the Mission Plan for them, and then roll them out in Mission Management and Mission Meetings. We both felt the crew would respond positively to this exciting and rewarding innovation.

WRITING THE CHECKS

"But this is just the beginning, Tom. With cash flow up to date, we can confidently look at writing the checks."

"Writing the checks. What's that?" Tom queried.

"This is one of the virtues of being on the Fourth Moon," I said. "With most businesses, the money is stuck in the business and never gets out. The owners have merely bought a job and are just earning a living. Cash flow is poorly managed. Suppliers aren't paid. It's a constant battle to survive.

"But owners that reach the Fourth Moon have their affairs in order. The business makes significant shareholder returns beyond the owner's operational salary. Cash flow is managed exceptionally well, working capital is maintained, and taxes are quarantined.

"You, Sarah, and the family can comfortably live off your operational salary of $200,000."

I watched Tom smile, and then continued. "Now we can finally plan to do something exciting that most owners don't do regularly, and that's write the checks. I even have a name for it: 'the check-writing ceremony.'

"I would suggest we hold a check-writing ceremony every quarter. This will eliminate any bumps or variances month-to-month. At the check-writing ceremony we review the net operating profit the business made in the prior quarter. With Day 15 dashboard reporting, the Profit & Loss reports will be available in the month following quarter-end, which would be October (September quarter), January (December quarter), April (March quarter), and July (June quarter).

"We would calculate 40% of the prior quarter's profits and ensure this is quarantined in the business tax bank account. I'd suggest transferring 40% of monthly profit each month as a discipline here to manage your cash flow. This covers the business tax payable."

Tom was listening intently, so I continued. "At the quarterly check-writing ceremony, you would therefore release 60% of the operating profit from the prior quarter as available for distribution. This amount would be payable to you and Sarah as the shareholders by check or bank transfer. Although I must say bank transfers aren't nearly as symbolic as writing a check to yourself.

"If we use last year's operating profit of $800,000, and assume an average quarterly profit of $200,000, the check-writing ceremony calculation would be:

Quarterly Operating Profit	**$200,000**
Less Tax Provision (40% of Operating Profit)	($80,000)
Check to Tom and Sarah	($120,000)

"This amount of $120,000 would be available to you and Sarah for personal use or investment purposes. It's as simple as that," I said.

"But what if there is no cash to pay it?" Tom queried.

"There will be. All your cash-flow provisions are up to date, and you have significant net receivables. That $500,000 of debtors' balances outstanding will be rolling in to your bank account in the next forty-five days. You can't go broke making a profit. The rules are simple: the cash-flow provisions must be maintained, and only the surplus (after-tax) profit can be withdrawn. If you don't make a profit for the quarter, there is no check-writing ceremony. If you make a loss for the quarter, that loss has to be recovered before the next quarter's check is written," I said.

"Okay, I get it," said Tom, who hadn't stopped smiling for a moment throughout this entire discussion.

THE POWER OF MULTIPLE INCOME STREAMS

I shared with Tom even more financial good news from his seat on Callisto. "The other Fourth Moon phenomenon is multiple income streams—in which you regularly receive money from multiple sources. Having multiple sources of earning capacity diversifies risk. Multiple revenue streams lead to more check-writing ceremonies. More revenue means bigger checks.

"When I met you, Tom, you had one primary revenue stream—from charging customers hourly for an IT consultant's time."

He nodded; I went on. "But now you have three branded software programs, three SLAs, consulting services, non-branded software sales, hardware sales, and specialist subcontractors you bring in on consulting projects. That totals ten. Ten revenue streams working for you.

"And that's just within Dylan IT. When we catch up next, we're going to explore building your empire. That's where we look at investing your quarterly checks in other vehicles for wealth creation. It could get pretty interesting for you and Sarah in the coming years."

Tom was excited at the prospect of creating wealth through other investments and revenue streams. He took a moment to privately congratulate himself on growing his revenue streams from just one to a whopping ten.

Tom was clearly reveling in Fourth Moon activities and looked forward to our next session when we would discuss wealth creation.

CHAPTER 21

Building Bigger Spaceships: Creating Wealth through Super Profits and Maximizing the Value of Your Business

"Creating wealth is what I want to talk about today, Tom. You've got to make some super profits, take action, and put your profits to work," I said as we started on our takeaway coffees in the Dylan IT boardroom.

"Super profits are just a name for making significant profits over and above your operational return. It's your investment return. Most businesses earn little or no investment return beyond their operational salary. As they utilize most or all of their operational salary on living expenses, there are often no significant investment returns to use for wealth creation. It's a six-figure investment return over and above your operational salary that provides the capital to create wealth. That's why I call them 'super profits.'

"So let's look at your super profits based on last year's investment return. The business generated an operating profit of $800,000. After deducting the

40% tax provision of $320,000, that leaves you with $480,000. I understand that you may earn more or less in the coming years, Tom, but I think we should use this investment return as a working number for our analysis. Are you comfortable with that?"

"I agree," he said. "I think it's doable. We achieved it, and my expectations are to maintain or better it. So yeah, let's use it," Tom said encouragingly.

"In addition to next year's after-tax profit, projected to be $480,000, you and Sarah have the surplus $200,000 you squirreled away from last year as a base," I reminded Tom.

"For modeling purposes, let's use the $480,000 as a working number after tax provisions are put aside. Keeping it simple and ignoring quarterly variations, this averages $120,000 per quarter. How do you feel about considering this $120,000 quarterly for investment?"

"I'm keen to look at that," Tom said brightly. "My $200,000 salary more than pays for living and lifestyle. Of the $120,000 predicted to be available at the check-writing ceremony each quarter, I'd like to take out $10,000 and add that to the $50,000 education fund we established for Jackson and Tyler. I would also like to take out an additional $10,000 each quarter and put it into cash for Sarah and me. Let's call that rainy-day money. So after those two $10,000 amounts are deducted, we're left with $100,000 each quarter, which I'm happy to invest."

"Great, Tom," I said. "That sounds considered and sensible. So looking at the residual $100,000 that you'll have for investment purposes each quarter, that equates to $400,000 per annum. That's a good investment funding pool, and more than meets the requirements of what I refer to as super profits.

"The next element to creating wealth is taking action. It sounds obvious, but you'd be surprised at how few people take action. They are in a position to invest, but for some reason they get distracted, allow doubt to creep in, or simply fail to execute. People who take action create wealth. It's as simple as that. Sure, it depends on investment choices and asset selection, but you have to actually take action, execute, and pull the trigger for wealth to accumulate. If someone sets a goal to buy a house every year over a decade but misses three years, he's still got seven houses at the end of the decade. The person who thinks about doing it but doesn't has none.

"The other aspect of wealth creation I wanted to explore is time in the market. Time in the market is the number of years that your investment has to appreciate and grow in value. A twenty-year-old who inherits a house has forty years of capital appreciation (and rental income on top of it) on that property by the time she turns sixty. A fifty-year-old purchasing property only has ten years of capital appreciation before turning sixty. Time in the market is critical to your wealth creation. It's never too late to start, but starting earlier makes you richer."

"So to sum up," clarified Tom, "I look likely to have super profits available for investment. I need to take action to get in the game, accumulate assets, and create wealth. And finally, I need to allow my investments to have time in the market to grow in value in order to multiply my wealth."

"Well said, Tom. That's exactly what we're doing as we build your empire."

CHOOSING THE RIGHT INVESTMENT VEHICLE

"I'm not a financial planner or investment adviser, nor your accountant," I said. "So I recommend you consider getting professional advice in the area of investment choice. However, what I can do is workshop some of those choices with you at a conceptual level.

"Let's look at this broadly in terms of passive investment and direct investment. Passive investment is where you invest passively with no direct involvement in the management of the investment. Direct investment is where you invest directly and participate actively in the investment.

"Passive investments might include investing in listed public shares or property trusts on one of the stock exchanges.

"Direct investments might include vertical integration within Dylan IT, where you introduce new business units to complement your existing product and service offerings. Alternatively, you may consider investing in other businesses in an executive or non-executive capacity. You may decide that you wish to get into real estate development, where you purchase property and improve the property through developing it for future resale. These direct investments generally require you to have some hands-on involvement in activities, even in a minor capacity. You wouldn't be entirely passive in your involvement."

Tom agreed to speak with advisers in the months ahead and to update me on his investment strategy prior to taking any action.

"How much is enough?" I asked Tom.

"What do you mean?" he asked.

"Well, we're not deciding on investments just yet, but it would be nice to explore some long-term investment goals. How much money do you really want?" I posed.

"I've never really thought about that. But I'm about to turn forty, so Sarah and I were discussing a ten-year plan to age fifty. Indulge me, Darren; how might that look?"

I calculated that if Tom invested $400,000 annually at an average compounding return of 8%, he'd accumulate just under $7 million by age fifty. To be conservative, I then used a 5% compounding rate, which equated to approximately $5.3 million. I settled on $6 million for discussion purposes.

Based on annual maintainable earnings of $1 million in ten years' time, and notwithstanding a decade of building his presence in his niche in growing the business, Tom could potentially estimate that a buyer might pay $4 million for the business, inclusive of the intellectual property on the niche products. Tom might be able to negotiate a percentage of ongoing royalties on branded product sales—let's say 5%. Based on last year's sales of $1 million on the three niche software programs, that would equate to an annual royalty of $50,000.

"Let's imagine, Tom, that you established $6 million in investment assets over the decade and then sold your business for $4 million. Ignoring tax implications, this would give you a net worth, excluding the family home, of $10 million. If you merely invested the $10 million for a 5% return, you'd generate $500,000 passive income per annum. When added to your $50,000 product royalty, this would total $550,000 per annum. Remember, this is totally passive income. You simply can't spend that sort of money. Despite what you'd spend of the $550,000 per annum, you'd still have the $10 million of investment assets accumulated untouched."

Tom looked at me in astonishment. While he had enjoyed making a huge profit last year, he hadn't considered the long-term impact of investing wisely, or the sort of wealth it could create over the next ten years for him, Sarah, and the kids. His mind had leapt ahead to a grand vision. He realized this was possible and not just a pipe dream. The Fourth Moon was a paradise of unlimited fortunes for those who could reach it, he thought to himself.

MAXIMIZING THE VALUE OF YOUR BUSINESS

Tom spoke up. "I broadly understand the compounding impact of my investment plan over a decade, but how do I work on maximizing the sale price of my business?" He was cleverly seizing on how he might influence his wealth creation journey even further.

"That's an important question you ask, Tom," I said. "If you understand the drivers that increase the value a prospective buyer is prepared to pay for your business, you can incorporate these factors into your strategy and business philosophy.

"Broadly speaking, there are two main ways to value a private business. The net-assets basis and net-earnings basis. The net-assets basis is simply the market value of the business's underlying assets less any liability outstanding on those underlying assets. A property trust that holds numerous property assets would be an example where this basis is used. However, for the vast majority of trading businesses, the net-earnings basis of valuation would be applied. Dylan IT would be valued on this basis using the business's EBIT (earnings before interest and tax) and applying a valuation multiple. For your purposes, EBIT would equate to your operating profit. For simplicity, let's assume a future maintainable operating profit of $1 million. An earnings multiple is simply the actual number of those maintainable annual profit (EBIT) values a prospective buyer is prepared to pay. For example, if a buyer is prepared to pay a four times multiple on an EBIT of $1 million, they're valuing the business at $4 million."

"So," Tom clarified, "you want to increase EBIT and the valuation multiple, as both of these input variables increase the business value?"

"Spot on," I said.

"So take me through some ways in which I can increase EBIT and the valuation multiple in the years ahead," Tom said.

"Okay, let's start with customers. Buyers like to see a diverse range of customers with established spending histories over a long period of time. Even better if contractual agreements are in place, Tom. Buyers are looking for barriers that prevent customers from leaving you.

"Key-person reliance is another factor. Buyers like to see that the business has a brand, and operates independently of the owner. Having strong, established management and a dedicated, experienced team on the ground helps. If key personnel are committed to staying with the business post-sale, this influences value also."

"I can see you've helped me on that one in putting the management team in place," Tom acknowledged.

"A strong foothold in your market also influences value," I said. "If Dylan IT is a leader in your market niche and your market niche is appealing, buyers will pay more.

"A consistent and predictable trading history is paramount," I continued. "Buyers look at your last three years' trading history as a minimum. You want solid historical trading profits in the years preceding a sale."

"That's good," Tom said supportively, "because our profitability should be relatively predictable from now on."

"And of course," I added, "a diversified product and service offering is beneficial. Buyers look at the sales mix of your revenue base. If they can see strong diversification, this may reduce their perceived risk, which increases value.

"Intangible assets such as intellectual property (IP) and patents and trademarks are often highly sought after. For example, if your products become well-known brands in your niche over time, buyers might pay more for ownership of this IP. The royalties we used in your net worth analysis were based on selling an IP asset."

"So my industry software could become valuable in time?" Tom asked.

"That's right, Tom. Especially if you have a strong market presence in your niche. There are many factors involved, but those give you an idea of what factors influence a business valuation. So in summary, create strong maintainable profits and a higher valuation multiple by addressing the factors I covered.

"There's been a lot to absorb in all this, Tom. I want to extend this conversation next time we meet up to cover the future scenarios in staying in the business or getting out. Don't worry. I'm not suggesting you're selling tomorrow. Michael Gerber, in his top-selling book, *The E-Myth*, called this 'preparing the business for sale.' If you can work on preparing the business for sale in the years ahead, it will position you ideally to maximize your sale value when you're ready to exit."

"So it's not about whether you intend to sell the business or not; it's the philosophy of preparing the business for sale so that when circumstances change, you're always immediately poised to take action and optimize your sale price," Tom said.

"Exactly, Tom," I said, nodding.

Tom and I finished our coffees while chatting about his racehorse's chances at Caulfield Racecourse on Saturday.

CHAPTER 22

Keep Flying or Sell the Spaceship: Continuance, Exit, and the Retirement Fallacy

"How exciting was it seeing my horse win at Caulfield?" Tom recalled excitedly.

"Jackson or Tyler could have ridden him on Saturday, Tom," I said. "He was just too good."

"You didn't tell me how exciting racing could be! A winning racehorse owners' dinner is hard to beat. It was funny seeing Sarah dancing with our jockey at the restaurant. What a night. She had a ball. The only problem is she expects every horse we own to be a winner now."

"They all do, Tom. It's all about managing expectations," I said, laughing.

I wanted to extend our previous discussion on business valuation factors into the decision-making criteria for staying in the business, or exiting.

I reminded Tom that his time on the Fourth Moon, which would be plentiful, was about getting out Galileo's telescope and taking a long-range view of the universe. Fourth Moon thinking is about planning, considering contingencies, maximizing gains, and locking in a worthwhile future. It's about leveraging your life.

Owners who reach the Fourth Moon are naturally curious souls. They have an appetite for knowledge and a strong desire to understand the principles and challenges they'll face long before they have to deal with such issues. This allows them valuable time to process the potential variables and apply rational problem-solving thinking within the safe confines of the Fourth Moon. Without external factors or real-time forces, they're able to work through many of the permutations and combinations to arrive at a current-view position. This current-view position is what they would do in the circumstances if they were making that decision today. They are then simply able to adjust their position as new factors emerge. This is an example of leverage on the Fourth Moon. Once the current view is established, the business owner only has to deal with new factors or changing circumstances to adjust his or her position. The bulk of the analysis and thinking has already been done.

This logic applied equally to Tom thinking about his intentions for the future. Rather than not consider his options and how to optimize his position in the future, he would simply analyze these issues now, long in advance of the event actually happening in the future.

So let's look at some scenarios Tom might face in the future. Firstly, Tom could stay in the business as a majority shareholder. We'll call this "continuance." Secondly, Tom might entirely exit the business, selling 100% of the business to a third party. We'll call this "exit." Thirdly, Tom might exit fully or partially by relinquishing control to a non-arm's-length party such as family or management. We'll call this "staged succession."

CONTINUANCE

Tom's first option is to make no change at all. He and Sarah can remain 100% shareholders and enjoy earning all of the business profits. Based on last financial year's profit of $800,000, let's say Tom can grow that to $1 million or beyond. The current option of having access to $1 million of total earnings each year indefinitely is an attractive one.

Tom's second option in the future might be to sell a minority shareholding up to 49% to an external third party. This would provide Tom and Sarah with an influx of sale proceeds that could be invested as part of their overall wealth creation plan. The minority shareholder(s) could be passive or operationally involved. If operationally involved, they may bring in management skills to reduce operational reliance on Tom. Further, they may have expertise that either grows the existing business more rapidly, or introduces new business opportunities to Tom that he previously didn't have access to.

Tom's third option under continuance might be to sell a minority shareholding to some or all of the management team. This is often called a management buyout, or MBO. The MBO could be staged over a number of years to allow management team members to fund their acquisition. For example, Jimmy, Livy, Willy, and Charlie might be invited to purchase a 2% shareholding each year over five years. After five years, each of them would own 10% of the business (40% held between them), with Tom and Sarah retaining a 60% shareholding. An MBO would help lessen Tom's operational accountability over time, as the MBO effectively locks in the retention of the MBO participants.

EXIT

Tom has the option in the future to sell 100% of the business to an arm's-length third party and exit fully.

Regardless of whether Tom advertises the business for sale or a prospective buyer approaches Tom with a sale offer, the exit option normally includes the business valuation factors of EBIT and a valuation multiplier being applied. For example, a buyer might apply a four times valuation multiplier on a $1 million EBIT to value the business at $4 million.

There may be enterprise value added to the business valuation for goodwill, intellectual property, or other intangible assets. Tom may negotiate a higher sale price for his branded niche software programs, which are his IP, or request an ongoing royalty (5% for example) on future product sales.

Tom should consider that the purchase of his business would generally require him to continue working in the business post-sale for a period of time. This might be six to eighteen months. Tom would generally be paid a generous consulting fee for providing these services post-sale. However, in their decision making under this scenario, Tom and Sarah should plan for Tom having a post-sale commitment.

SUCCESSION

Tom has the option in the future to look at succession through non-arm's-length parties.

Tom and Sarah could transfer their shareholding to family members. At this stage, the children, Jackson and Tyler, are minors. However, in ten to fifteen years they'll be young adults who may want to join the family business and ultimately run it one day.

Referring back to the management buyout (MBO) discussed earlier, Tom may alternatively decide to offer the MBO participants an opportunity to purchase 100% of the business. This could be staged and timed to the satisfaction of Tom and Sarah as well as the MBO participants.

THE RETIREMENT FALLACY

"It's helpful," Tom began, "to think ahead in regard to all the options I have available. What's reassuring is I don't have to decide anything in the immediate future. I never thought there were so many ways to sell a business, let alone the multitude of factors that influence valuation. The Fourth Moon's got me learning and thinking more about my options," Tom said reflectively.

"There's one more thing I want to share with you about staying in or getting out, Tom. It's what I call 'the retirement fallacy.'

"Think of a large circle, and right inside it are all of the options you have in the future including continuance, exit, or succession. The circle represents your overall perspective and personal factors affecting the decision you'll ultimately make.

"The circle surrounds your options. It's the sum of you. It includes your age, as this will influence your timing and choices. It includes your health, as health is always a shaper of decisions. It includes wealth. It also includes desire and state of mind. Desires and motivations change over time, and these certainly impact the timing and choices in your decision making."

Tom took a turn now. "So while I can learn and define the choices I might have available to me in staying in or getting out, the personal and subjective factors of age, health, wealth, and psychological state are more experiential. I have to experience how I will feel in the future. I simply can't predict that accurately, can I, Darren?"

"No, you can't, Tom. That's the mysterious bit."

"The retirement fallacy I refer to is a close cousin of the work paradigm. You remember me talking about the five-day workweek, which seems to have blown out in private business to see owners working 7 AM to 7 PM each day? When you have worked from 7 AM to 7 PM every workday until you're old, you get to retire. When you retire, you get to stop working and do very little. The notion seems to be that you've done your bit, so we don't expect you to produce any more.

"Retirement is a fallacy to me," I went on, "because if we control our own destiny, why do we have to stop doing the things we love? We are living longer, medical science keeps us healthier longer into life, and technology allows us to be part of a global village no matter where we are in the world.

"Individuals who reach the Fourth Moon develop relationships and interests long before they grow old. The leverage offered on the Fourth Moon provides the time and environment to create other pursuits outside your core business.

"On the Fourth Moon, there is no such thing as stereotypical retirement. Business owners might sell their business but engage themselves purposefully in many other activities long into old age. The recognition that retirement is a fallacy keeps them vital and engaged in life. Fourth Moon thinking contributes to longevity."

I explained to Tom that we'd workshop some strategies for developing his Fourth Moon psyche at our next meeting. I suggested a different environment might complement our session, so we agreed to meet in the beautiful seaside town called Mount Martha, located on the Mornington Peninsula outside of Melbourne.

CHAPTER 23

Orbiting Secrets:
Advanced Fourth Moon Habits

It was a perfect autumn morning in Mount Martha, a picturesque seaside village. Tom and I had met for breakfast at OB's Café, and it wasn't long before we were tucking in to bacon, eggs, corn fritters, and smashed avocado. The glow of the morning sun and smell of salt air coming off the sea provided the perfect backdrop for some lateral thinking.

"I talked last time about developing passions outside of the business. I call these 'loves and lifestyle.' Loves and lifestyle often can't enter your life fully before the Fourth Moon. Stuff just can't get in. No doubt some things can, but certainly not abundance. It's like a vacuum exists within your business life and it blocks a lot of the good stuff out. On the Fourth Moon this vacuum is released, and suddenly all that abundance rushes in. I remember listening with great interest as you explained how much your personal life has changed. Your relationship with Sarah, Jackson, and Tyler. The revitalization of your relationship with your parents. The reconnection with old friends and the openness to new ones. Your sports, hobbies, and travel. What about your charity work? The list is endless.

"You didn't just fluke this, Tom. Nor did you do it mechanically off a checklist. You did it because you've changed. You did it because you have a new lens on the Fourth Moon. You did it from the heart. I encourage you to continue to focus on loves and lifestyle in your life. You've started; you've embraced it. Now you must continue it indefinitely. Share this discussion with Sarah, and ask her to remind you of it if she ever sees you dropping back to old-world habits."

Tom agreed. "I feel like I've got a new set of eyes. A new lens, as you put it. I'm not going back to old ways. I can assure you of that," Tom said confidently.

"Let's get on to some non-surgical enhancements, Tom. Regular refreshing of your body and mind is another Fourth Moon habit. Let me refer to a quick story to demonstrate this.

"There were two lumberjacks that made a bet as to which one of them could cut down the most trees in a day. One of them was a huge brute of a man, nearly 350 pounds, or 160 kilograms, while the other was a smaller, leaner man weighing just 175 pounds, or 80 kilograms. At dawn they started their competition, having agreed to finish cutting trees at sunset. The larger man went out hard and chopped down trees for five hours straight without stopping for even a brief moment. In contrast, the smaller man went slowly but purposefully about his work. Every hour he stopped to sharpen his saw and take water. As the midday sun climbed to the peak of the sky and the mercury rose, the larger man fell down to the ground exhausted, his saw blades worn down to nothing. He looked over at the small man with pity in his eyes. 'I've cut down over twenty trees, and you've done half that,' he said, laughing. The smaller man looked up calmly and said, 'But it's still six hours until sunset. I have energy and a sharp saw.'

"You can guess who won the bet," I quipped.

"You've been sharpening the saw also, Tom. Reduced hours, delegation, no working late at home, and the six weeks of holidays. I'm impressed you're taking some Fridays off next year from the business to pursue other interests. Consider improving your diet, getting massage, practicing meditation, and increasing sleeping hours, and you'll be better prepared for a sustained future.

"Another non-surgical enhancement is reinvention. In this world of constant change, we've all got to reinvent ourselves every three to five years, just to keep our edge. Reinventing yourself is about committing to learning for life. And it is generally outside your typical field of expertise. It's about unleashing the curious child within and acknowledging that you are much more than your business nametag suggests. The world loves reinvention. The nanny turns into a crime novelist. Bookkeeper becomes boutique dressmaker. Lawyer becomes horse trainer. Today's world allows you to reinvent yourself. It might even expect you to. Study philosophy or a language. Build those hardwood, handmade tables you've always dreamt of. You always discover something new about yourself through reinvention.

"A by-product is that you become better at your core discipline. Reinventing seems to make you more well-rounded and helps you incorporate the knowledge of new skills into your old skill set. It's like adding new tools to your existing toolkit.

"Innovation is another non-surgical enhancement on the Fourth Moon. The Fourth Moon provides the ideal environment to create more right-brain thinking. The leverage of the Fourth Moon creates time for you to become more innovative. But remember, Tom, to fail fast. Don't spend endless time and money on something that could risk the farm. Never bet the farm. Instead, make small, calculated bets that don't risk everything. Make small bets that have upside with low risk, and learn to fail fast so you can move on to other projects. Pixar and Apple have learnt to fail fast so they can move on to their next winning project."

"I like the sound of having time to make those non-surgical enhancements," Tom said in a measured tone. "I think I've developed loves and lifestyle over the last twelve months, and I'm getting better at refreshing. I think I need to turn my mind now to reinventing and innovating."

"I want to come back now to the discipline of orbiting all four moons," I said.

"Okay," said Tom, concentrating.

"This is perhaps the most important discipline. I talked about it very early on in your journey, and you've been so busy pushing forward, there was no point in discussing going back.

"But on the Fourth Moon we need to commit to going back whenever needed to revisit the first three moons.

"If you decide on the Fourth Moon that you need to change an existing strategy or introduce a new strategy, you must go back to the First Moon and develop this strategy.

"You then need to go on to the Second Moon and implement this strategy. This might include updating the Mission Plan or adding a new project. It could involve updating a key business system or adjusting your dashboard reporting.

"Having implemented the strategy, you move on to the Third Moon and determine how you will maintain the Mission Plan. This might involve observing this in a Mission Meeting, monitoring it with the crew member accountable, or reviewing a periodic report.

"You can then return back to the Fourth Moon, having orbited the three other moons to strategize, implement, and maintain the initiative."

"How often will this happen, Darren?" Tom asked.

"As seldom or as often as it needs to. You'll know, Tom. And so will we."

"Who's we?" Tom asked curiously.

"Remember you have a crew now. I'll be here with you at a senior strategic level to monitor the orbiting of the moons. The management team will provide important feedback operationally through Mission Meetings and Mission Management as well as their individual Crew Reviews with you. And finally, the wider crew on the ground will provide broader feedback from the customer interface.

"This internal feedback mechanism is complemented by the wide-ranging external feedback mechanism you have in place with your other stakeholders, your customers, and your suppliers. Those forums will provide the insight you need to make the required changes to strategy. And don't forget Sarah; you've asked her to be your compass as the shareholder stakeholder in all this, too."

CHAPTER 24

Reflections from Callisto

Tom and I stood on the rooftop of Dylan IT's offices. Having raised a toast to Dylan IT, we gazed upward silently and watched the moon rise for the evening.

Let us return to Galileo for a moment.

Galileo's proof that the geocentric theory was false, that everything in the universe did not in fact revolve around the earth, signified a profound moment in history. The geocentric view was universally accepted for centuries. While Copernicus challenged it prior to Galileo, his findings were based on mathematical calculations that could not be definitively proven.

The desire to maintain the geocentric view goes to the very emotional core of humanity—the ego. There is an overwhelming human desire to be exceptional. Our sense of belonging, purpose, and motivation was more easily driven by the belief that we, and only we, were the center of the cosmos.

The effects of Galileo's irrefutable proof had an alarming and far-reaching impact on society in that time. The belief that everything in the universe revolved around us and that we were the center of the universe was a paradigm that the collective ego must have found incredibly difficult to give up.

Tom had been prepared to dismiss his old worldview. Initially it had been overwhelming. He even resisted for a while. But Tom came to embrace a new philosophy and set off on his journey to the Fourth Moon. Like Galileo's discovery, his decision to adopt a new paradigm was vindicated by the ultimate proof—success.

You, just like Tom, do not need to overcome the challenges that Galileo faced. You merely need to review your own business paradigm through a new lens. If humankind's collective ego was able to surrender the belief of being the center of the universe, surely you can surrender a paradigm that is holding you back from more success and happiness in your business and personal life.

Only you can ultimately change your paradigm. Anyone willing to follow Tom on his journey and embrace the principles outlined in this book can reach the Fourth Moon.

The Fourth Moon is vast, abundant, and lightly populated. It is rich in resources, and there is more than enough room for all of us. Visitors to the Fourth Moon love life, laugh louder, and live longer.

If you've read this far, I trust you've already commenced your journey. I urge you to continue and not give up. There will be obstacles and setbacks, I assure you, as there are on any great pilgrimage. Don't grow old living with regret. Better to have exhausted yourself trying than live in the gray twilight of having never dared. Please don't die wondering.

Push forward. One step at a time. Commit to the forever disciplines required.

Reach the Fourth Moon.

Acknowledgments

To my parents, Kevin and Barbara. You taught me the ethics and values I carry each day. Thank you for loving me, educating me, and nurturing self-belief.

Professionally, thank you, Vin, for looking after the young bull. Thank you to Stephen, Mark, and Don, and to the firm of Pitcher Partners.

To all my amazing clients, thank you for allowing me to work together with you and participate in our business playground. Without you, there is no game to play.

To Greenleaf Book Group, I truly appreciate the encouragement and guidance from you in getting my vision into print.

And finally, sincere thanks to my wonderful army of family and friends for your continued interest, support, and loyalty.

Fourth Moon Resources:
Start Your Journey Now

FOUR RESOURCES TO HELP YOU LAUNCH

Are you ready to take your journey to the Fourth Moon? Here are the essential resources to get you off the ground.

Read the Fourth Moon Blog.

Get free tools, tips, and techniques to support you on your journey to the Fourth Moon. www.thefourthmoon.com.

Join the Fourth Moon Community.

Join the Fourth Moon online community and comment with us through your favorite social media:

- Twitter: @DarrenKBourke
- Facebook: Facebook.com/DarrenKBourke
- YouTube: youtube.com/user/DarrenKBourke
- LinkedIn: au.linkedin.com/in/darrenkbourke

Get Your Free Extract from Fourth Moon Mastery.

Download your free digital training extract and prepare for liftoff at www.thefourthmoon.com.

Accelerate to the Fourth Moon.

Fourth Moon Mastery is the easiest—and fastest—way to reach the Fourth Moon. This digital training program is the complete and comprehensive step-by-step guide to achieving optimal and sustainable success that any business can follow.

In this training, Darren Bourke will guide you step-by-step through the process from First Moon to Fourth Moon. The detailed content is immediately implementable, can be worked on at your own pace, and is easy to access on your desktop or tablet.

The Fourth Moon Mastery digital program includes video, audio, documentation, templates, tools, and resources that will teach and guide you to reach the Fourth Moon.

For complete details of Fourth Moon Mastery, go to: www.thefourth moon.com.

Photograph by Steven Pam

About the Author

Darren Bourke is a consultant, coach, and mentor to small and medium-sized businesses. With more than twenty-five years of business experience, he has an intuitive understanding of what makes entrepreneurs and businesses succeed. He has worked with nearly a thousand businesses throughout his career.

A chartered accountant by profession, Darren's entrepreneurial journey kicked off when he jointly founded a start-up permanent and contract placement recruitment agency, hiring hundreds of finance and management personnel for clients. His unique combination of financial, management, people, and business skills then led him to create Business Influence, where he specializes in coaching businesses.

When he's not spending time with family and friends, Darren's alpha-male passion for "Australian rules" football and thoroughbred racing is complemented by his sensitive, new age love of music, film, theater, literature, and wine.

A screenwriting course led to his lightbulb moment of combining a love of business and a love of writing through the storytelling metaphor adopted in *The Fourth Moon.*

Darren lives in Melbourne, Australia, with his wife and two children. Visit him at www.darrenkbourke.com.